THE JOY OF BEING

Supporting hardworking mums
to stress less & live more

MARINA PEARSON

The Joy of Being

Supporting hardworking mums to stress less & live more

First published in 2019 by
Panoma Press Ltd
48 St Vincent Drive, St Albans, Herts, AL1 5SJ UK
info@panomapress.com
www.panomapress.com

Cover design by Neil Coe
Artwork by Karen Gladwell

ISBN 978-1-784521-61-5

Printed and bound in Great Britain by TJ International Ltd, Padstow

*To my son Leo and all the hardworking
mums in the world who are doing an
amazing job in bringing up their kids and
making stuff happen.*

What People are Saying:

"The Joy of Being is unlike any other self-improvement book out there! The revolutionary understanding that Marina writes about for hardworking mums will have you fall back in love with life and work in no time."

Ella Louise Woodhouse
Mum and CEO, Elle Entertainment

"Marina's written a book that is a gift for any woman, especially mums, who want to step off the treadmill of incessant thinking and doing to experience true inner peace. That's a bold statement, but not only is The Joy of Being packed full of wisdom and insight, more importantly, Marina provides a roadmap for connecting with your own inner wisdom and insight, so that no matter what your current conditions seem like, you can find a way to the life experience you desire. Well done, Marina. You've made an important and significant contribution to the lives of many women (and men!)."

Bernadette Doyle
Transformation Business Mentor

"The Joy of Being is a real gift to working mothers... It shows how it really is possible to combine work and parenting from a sweeter, calmer place."

Lian Brook-Tyler

Mother, Co-Founder and Podcast Host of *Primal Happiness*

"In this beautiful guide to living more and stressing less, Marina shows that these moments of deep stillness, grace and joy do not need to happen by chance. Instead there is a path each of us can follow and access whenever we choose."

Ann Wilson

Bestselling Hay House author of *The Wealth Chef* and entrepreneur

"A wonderfully insightful book from a woman who is a true joy to be around. If you want a life filled with love, joy and abundant blessings, The Joy of Being is filled with common sense advice, humorous and insightful anecdotes, and a fresh perspective on life that may well lead you to it."

Mamoon Yusaf

Bestselling Author of *Inside the Soul of Islam*

Acknowledgements

I would love to acknowledge all the teachers who have pointed me in the right direction, showing me how life works. Special thanks to Jamie Smart for being the reason I started looking in this direction in the first place, who has been an amazing guide during this process. To Jan and Chip Chipman who have sat for endless hours listening to my misguided rants and gently pointed me back "home". To Michael Neill whose words always have an impact. To Ann Wilson for writing the foreword and whose wise counsel has helped me set up my finances in such a way that I have been able to write this book without needing to work.

My deep gratitude to my son Leo, my biggest teacher, who has woken me up on countless occasions and without whom this book wouldn't have been written.

To my dear friends, Rose Anne and Phil, who have been steadfast supporters of my work and listened in on numerous meltdowns.

I would also love to thank all of those who read the book and commented on where I could improve it and bring it alive.

To all my clients who have contributed to this book's stories and who have the courage to step up and out every day. Thank you for the inspiration that you bring to everyone around you.

Finally, a big thank you to Mindy and the team at Panoma Press for publishing this book and getting the word out. And to Wendy Millgate-Stuart of Wendy & Words for her detailed copyediting. A big thank you to my close family for their support and the joy that they bring to my world.

Foreword

Perhaps it's the riff of your favourite rock anthem.

Perhaps it's the rhythmic scraping of waves rolling up a sandy beach.

Perhaps it's the sound of the breath of a beloved sleeping.

Perhaps it's wind rustling through a forest.

Perhaps it's something altogether different for you.

It's that place, that sound, that moment where everything is still.

Not a 'dead, nothing's happening here' kind of still.

More an 'everything's happening here and nothing is missing' kind of still.

It's the eye of the storm kind of still.

We all know it, even if it's only a fleeting, distant kind of knowing.

It's deeply familiar and deeply nourishing.

Whatever it is for you,

… it's the vibration of joy.

It's the essence of being… it's the place that Marina has found her way to.

In this beautiful guide to living more and stressing less, Marina shows that these moments of deep stillness, grace and joy do not need to happen by chance. Instead, there is a path each of us can follow and access whenever we choose.

She shows that you don't have to go to the top of a mountain to check out of your life on an *Eat, Pray, Love* pilgrimage to experience this.

Whether tripping over Lego blocks, mopping up dog vomit, directing a team or churning out an overdue business report, there is a way to come back to joy, and this book shows us the way.

Ann Wilson,

Bestselling Hay House author of
***The Wealth Chef* and entrepreneur**

Preface

Gosh, I wish I didn't feel so stressed. I have so much on my plate at the moment that I can't see the wood for the trees. I wish I could just switch off and have more time for me.

This is how conversations with myself used to go when I was working 60 hours a week, rushing in and out of London and running from meeting to meeting. Most of the time it felt as if I were going uphill with the brakes on and I wished I could just stop and find a more effortless way to live.

For about 10 years I had been working in the personal development industry, both from a coaching perspective and on my own development. I was on a constant search and striving to work on myself and it felt that what I was learning was never quite enough. Somewhere deep inside, I knew that there was a truth I wasn't seeing – something I hadn't quite bumped into, but knew would help me live the life of peace and calm I secretly yearned for.

Then that day came.

I remember it clearly. It was the day I was about to stop coaching and leave the industry *forever*. The message came in the form of a Facebook post that stopped me in my tracks:

> "And in this game of life, we all search for ourselves. When I say selves, I mean 'inner selves', the thing that creates the life in the place. Now consciously, most of us are not aware of this. But if you are searching for happiness; if you're searching for tranquillity; if you're searching just to have a nice, peaceful, loving, understanding life... in actual fact, you're searching for your inner self." SYDNEY BANKS

In that moment, my mind settled down and I became very still. I saw that what I had been looking for had been under my nose the entire time. It was within me. I could stop the search.

From then on, I became curious about this way of viewing life and started to investigate the understanding that I now share with my clients – hardworking mums who either own a business or who have a demanding job. As I kept exploring, I noticed that I was experiencing a greater sense of peace and joy more of the time. Much of the overthinking and worry that had housed itself like an unwanted guest for so many years continued to fall away.

The unfamiliar sensation, created by the dropping away of my constant insecure thinking, felt deeply uncomfortable. I felt naked. Over time, however, I have come to experience this stillness and peace as something that I can rely on and work with. The outcome has been and continues to be a richer, fuller experience of life. It gives me the greatest satisfaction to help other hardworking mums to achieve this too. To stress less, live more and Be in Joy.

Contents

Introduction

If you have ever wondered how it's possible to create an extraordinary and fulfilling life, where joy doesn't exist as an afterthought but is at the centre of your everyday life, you are in the right place. I know it may be hard to understand how it's possible to experience fulfilment and satisfaction that already exists regardless of your circumstances. Having lived from a place of frustration and overwhelm for so long, this may well be a foreign concept to you. But my intent is that once you have read this book, it won't be any longer!

Unlike most personal development books that focus on what you need to do in order to experience joy, I will be sharing the understanding of how we each experience life and my insights around the subject, for you to have your own realisations.

I am aware that the way I see the subject of joy may change over time, and right now I am sharing my current version of how I see it. Before I go into more detail, I'd like to take you on a journey from where you may be right now to where you want to go.

If you are a busy, hardworking mum who runs a business or has a demanding job, if you struggle to feel grateful for what you have as you spend most of your time in stress, worry, guilt and general malaise, this book is for you.

You may find switching off from your problems difficult to achieve. Perhaps you are kept up at night attempting to figure out how you're going to get everything done. Maybe you worry that you feel unsatisfied with your life and wonder whether it has to do with your business, your partner (or lack of partner), your kids, your clients or the fact that you have neglected yourself and constantly give to others. You cannot quite put your finger on it and worry that this feeling will live with you for the rest of your life. You know you should feel grateful and yet you beat yourself up because you don't experience more gratitude.

You hustle, keep busy and do the hard work, because this is the only way you know how. You may even have moments where you ask yourself *What is the point?* as you compare yourself to others who are more successful than you, prettier than you, richer than you – and the list goes on.

The pressures of work and management of your time are also something you struggle with, as you rush from meeting to meeting to get back home to look after those you love. You cannot remember the last time you took time out for you and actually enjoyed it. You prop yourself up with coffee to get through the day, and in the evening you may well have come to depend on that bottle of wine that softens the edges of difficult and challenging days.

You feel like a hamster on a wheel, but you can't get off. Not because you don't want to but because you don't know how. You may have read a ton of books on the subject, and you may have gone to yoga or meditation classes to calm your mind. Nothing has worked.

The constant search for peace and fulfilment is never-ending and exhausting. While you keep your game face on, you run on empty and wonder if it will ever change. This book will support you to experience life with joy, more of the time. After all, what is the point of being gifted life if you are not enjoying it?

The *Joy of Being* is an opportunity for you to see through the myths that have been holding you back from experiencing life the way you dream it could be. Imagine a life where *contentment* takes centre stage and where you can switch off with more ease. A life where you can make time for yourself and your self-care more often. A life where you spend little time comparing yourself to others and beating yourself up (metaphorically). A life where you prioritise spending time with the people you care about versus working yourself to the bone.

As you spend more of your time living like this, people comment on how much calmer and joyful you are. You pat yourself on the back because you know that this is really true. Long gone are the days when you thought that what you did, what you had or how much you earned said something about you. It has freed you up to enjoy your life and work in a way you never thought possible. Even difficult clients don't seem that difficult anymore, and the resentments you hold for those you love don't seem to be as overwhelming as they used to be.

In short, your experience of your life is one of more joy, fun and lightness!

My hope is that this book will be the spark – the catalyst toward the transformation you seek. This book is an invitation for you to look within, as so many of my mum clients have done already. You will find I use the expression 'insightfully see' on numerous occasions. This is an encouragement to see yourself and life with a new level of understanding and awareness, as you look inward. A new perspective. At the end of each chapter, I share a recap of the chapter's learnings to encourage self-reflection as you move forward.

I share my insights with you, so you too can experience your own path of least resistance and ultimate joy.

It is time for you to unplug from any insecurities that plague you and light up with the joy that already exists inside you. The Joy of Being is possible for everyone.

PART ONE
STRESS LESS

"Everybody in the world seeks happiness
whether they know it or not, because if they
ever find out how their mind works, this is
the first major step to happiness."

SYDNEY BANKS

CHAPTER ONE

Joy Exposed

"Joy is a natural phenomenon; misery is your creation."

SADHGURU

Did you know that everyone is born joyful?

Joy is our innate state, as is peace and contentment. When you are born, you have no pre-conceived ideas, beliefs, opinions or justifications about how the world works. Neither do you know who you are. As you are pure awareness, you merely observe. When judgments and analysis aren't present, that's when you experience joy. Some call it 'having presence of mind' or 'being in the present moment'.

You may currently be looking for it in a bottle of wine, in spending money, in your family or even in your work. You won't find it, however, because joy will never be found in these places, no matter how hard you search. One of the important implications of 'insightfully seeing' (gaining a new level of understanding and awareness) is that you spend less time innocently searching for joy in the wrong places.

Releasing insecure thoughts and behaviours

Insightfully seeing where joy comes from can help you drop unhelpful and insecure behaviours, thinking and attachments. For example, if you think someone else can give you the joy you seek when they are not around or they leave, it may seem that you are not able to cope because your security and wellbeing lies in being with them.

While it may appear that other people or your circumstances can give you a feeling of joy, and I know just how compelling this illusion is, it simply isn't the case. The important thing to understand is that we have assumed that the feeling is related to something 'outside ourselves' because the illusion is convincing. And just as the sun doesn't literally rise and set, but rather the Earth revolves around its axis, feelings don't come from your circumstances. You are only ever feeling the experience of thinking in the moment.

When you live less of your time in the intellect and don't give such importance to judgments and analysis, life becomes a magical journey you can savour and not something you need to figure out. As you continue to grow, you can navigate life with more ease because you are more in touch with your intuition. That's when you notice you no longer need to control your circumstances to feel happy because there is a knowing that joy exists inside.

If you don't know this, you may well be willing your circumstances to change so that you can experience the joy and happiness that you think comes from 'out there'.

For example, do you find yourself saying...

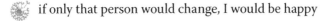 if only that person would change, I would be happy

if I only knew what was wrong, I would be happy

if only I didn't have so much to do, I would be happy

if only I could live my dream life, I wouldn't have to worry again and then I would be happy

if only I had more time to get everything done, I would be happy?

Or maybe you have your own: 'If only..., then...'

Most people think that having an amazing quality of life revolves around what they have, instead of how they are experiencing life. You may have a successful business, an amazing home, great kids or a fantastic team, but if you are not able to find joy in them, what's the point?

When you spend more time in your place of joy, you appreciate what you have so much more, and you tend to not take life so seriously. You listen to what your heart wants regardless of how crazy your ideas may seem. You spend more time on the projects and with the people that matter to you. You are better able to stand in your truth without compromise and feel far more connected to life as you don't take the thinking you experience as seriously. And you simply don't need to consider certain insecure thoughts. I can totally relate to this. I used to take my suicidal thoughts in earnest, but now I don´t.

At 21 I attempted suicide. I thought I had to believe what thought was telling me, which is why one day I decided to finally end my life. I'd had enough of living in the pain I was in.

Every day was a struggle to be happy, a struggle to be me, a struggle to be alive in this body I had been given. At the time I was taking drugs to numb the pain, but the comedowns were getting worse and worse, until it got so bad that I decided to put an end to my misery. I went to the pharmacy and bought a box of sleeping pills. Ten minutes later I walked into the kitchen, filled a glass with water and swallowed the entire packet. I lay on the bed awaiting my fate.

While I lay there, a new thought shouted at me to get out of bed and run downstairs for help. Instead of ignoring it, I realised in that moment that I wasn't ready to die. I needed help, fast. I found myself running downstairs into the living room and telling my flatmate to call an ambulance. Fifteen minutes later I was rushed to hospital where I had my stomach pumped. The next morning, my mother arrived and I left university to begin the healing process at home.

Since then I have had the odd moment of wanting to leave again, as I did during the separation from my ex-husband. But by then I was able to see the thoughts for what they were. I realised I didn't need to act on them. They were just patterns of thinking that had come to say hello. Nothing more.

Painful? Yes. But taking my life made no sense.

Ditch the 'seriousness' and avoid burnout

Did you know that you don´t need to believe your ¨difficult¨ thinking? Instead, you can approach life with more joy in your heart by understanding how the mind works.

I don't know about you, but I thought that in order to 'do' life properly as an adult, I had to believe every thought I had. Thanks to the accumulation of unhelpful thinking patterns, I experienced depressive thinking, suicidal thoughts and found life hard to navigate. It came as a huge relief to discover that joy is inside all of us. You don´t need to find it in some far-off destination. You can ˋliveˊ that joy now. You can ˋplayˊ. But I had to learn this after some big lessons.

Back in January 2013 I had just written a number one bestselling book called *Goodbye Mr Ex* and was about to get married. I lived in an amazing home in Hertfordshire and had been gifted an inheritance that my husband-to-be and I could have lived on comfortably for many years.

And yet I was stressed out and felt unfulfilled. I was so worried the money would run out as it was a finite pot. I wanted to prove to myself that I could make the money on my own. My worry about it running out consumed me and I found myself rushing into London for meetings to drum up more business. In hindsight, I was doing nothing more than keeping busy.

I would wake up exhausted every morning from the constant demands and pressures I was placing on myself to make more money and be more successful. I thought that once I had achieved business success from my coaching practice, I could just enjoy myself and the stress would go. Little did I know how this way of thinking was keeping me stuck on the hamster wheel of striving.

Every morning I felt as if I had been run over by a truck, feeling depleted, stressed and anxious. On paper, everything looked amazing, but it certainly didn't feel that way to me. I didn't understand why I felt the way I did and judged myself for feeling ungrateful and down. After all, I had everything I had ever dreamed of: a beautiful home, a successful fiancé, more than enough money in the bank and my health.

Like most of my clients, I thought my stress and lack of fulfilment were a result of external factors: my finances, the endless to-do list, not being a success, my partner, my colleagues, my inability to make my business work, the long hours I worked, investing money in the wrong deals, hiring the wrong people in the business, the lack of speaking engagements, not having enough impact on the world, lack of clients and, and, and! The list was endless.

My mind couldn't keep still and kept me up at night, putting a strain on my relationship with my fiancé.

Despite being at the height of my success with *Goodbye Mr Ex* and being featured in the top UK magazines, I was ready to quit. Like most of my clients, I felt trapped by my lifestyle and I was hating the journey. I had put aside all the things I loved doing and knew were good for me – yoga, singing and dancing – all in the hot pursuit of success, or at least the feeling of it. However, what I didn't know then was that no amount of searching for this feeling of success would bring it about.

Learning to slow down

When we decided to move to Bali, I couldn't have been happier. I thought *Well, at least now I won't be so stressed.* During the first couple of weeks, however, I realised that changing locations hadn't made any difference. I was stressed when I arrived in Bali, and I continued to work the same long hours as I had in the UK.

My experience of life had nothing to do with where I was living. It couldn't have because there I was, on the other side of the world, experiencing my world in the same stressful manner.

Six weeks after the move, I was stopped in my tracks: I was pregnant. This was the biggest gift as I had to slow down thanks to severe morning sickness and exhaustion. All I did for the next two months was rest and sleep.

This physical slowing down had a profound impact. I became aware of just how busy my mind was. Something else changed. Slowing down (or in this case stopping) was affecting my psyche. One of the simple questions that came to cement my direction was "Is it possible to live with more ease and joy regardless of the circumstances?"

And the answer? "Yes, it is!"

You see, if joy is what remains when judgment and analysis have fallen away, experiencing it has nothing to do with what you have or don't have. The implications of this are enormous. It means you are not beholden to circumstances or other people for giving you joy because they can't.

Over the past four years, I have been deepening my experience of joy and sharing my insights with clients. What I've seen time and again is that when they realise that they aren't at the mercy of their feelings being created by their conditions, they spend less time experiencing their life as if they were cycling uphill with the brakes on, as Michelle was.

Michelle's story

Michelle was one of my VIP clients. She was miserable when she first came to me. She was drinking every night and binge eating to cover her pain. Her marriage was on the rocks, and her business wasn't earning any money. Within nine months of working with me, her marriage was back on track and she had stopped the need to binge eat and drink. Over the years I have seen her relationship with her children grow and blossom. She now chooses to work on projects that light her up, while owning her talent as an artist that she had previously set aside. She realised that joy came from within and not from anything outside her.

If by reading this chapter, you think you are a long way from experiencing the joy you seek, think again. You may have been looking in the wrong direction. I will cover this in greater detail in the next chapter.

Let's recap and reflect

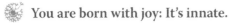 You are born with joy: It's innate.

External factors cannot give you a feeling.

When you look inside, you will find what you are looking for.

 You are free to feel joy regardless of your circumstances.

You don't need to take every thought you think seriously.

CHAPTER TWO

Re-thinking Negative Feelings

"All feeling is neutral until we judge it."

MARINA PEARSON

Just as you can misunderstand where joy comes from, the same can be said for so-called 'negative' feelings such as stress, anger, overwhelm and so on. When you have these feelings, do they give you a sense of not being able to cope with all your responsibilities? My clients share how their stress becomes stressful to live with and their emotional overwhelm becomes overwhelming.

The challenge isn't that you are experiencing insecure feelings. The obstacle is in believing that something other than thought is creating the feelings you experience. Likewise, judging the feelings you have as 'bad' while searching to get rid of them provides further challenge.

When you do this, it may look as if you have ever-increasing issues to solve and change: Life seems complex. You may spend your time worrying or overthinking things or ruminating over the 101 reasons why you feel the way you do – money, lack of time, difficult people, to-do lists, feeling tired, deadlines, team, juggling family or work – and what you need to change in order to feel better. This is exhausting and can deplete your energy. When you search to get rid of 'bad' feelings, it will inevitably keep you in the search and struggle for longer, moving you further away from the joy and peace you seek.

If you have never insightfully seen that you are living in the feeling of your thinking and not your circumstances, it can look as if you are a victim of those circumstances when you aren't. When you believe your thinking and emotional state work in a way that they do not (believing feelings come from the job, the hours, other people...), you may perceive you are a victim and you will experience feeling victimised. When this happens you are *experiencing thought*, living in the feeling of your thinking, which means you are actually not a victim of circumstance.

Stop managing the feelings you have

The most common way to try to relieve stress is to do something about it by managing it or getting rid of it. In other words, we fall into the trap of wanting to control our stress, so we can live with it or do something to make it stop. I have often seen rituals such as meditation, yoga, exercise or journaling being prescribed for stress. Now there is nothing wrong with any of these activities. They all have their place. But the challenge comes when you think that the reason you feel better is because of the activities that you take part in. If you are relying on these activities to give you a feeling of wellbeing, you are back in the illusion again. While these activities are helpful to maintain a healthy body, they cannot give you a feeling.

Let's take yoga as an example.

For the last 14 years I have practised Ashtanga yoga as a way to calm my mind. I initially used it to get to somewhere other than where I was, like most practitioners I knew. While yoga is an incredible way to look after the body and nurture it, the people I met who used it to de-stress were some of the most stressed people I have ever met. Me included! I was part of the group of people who came to yoga to escape their stress and used it as somewhere to get to – as an escape.

While there wasn't anything wrong with this, I was missing out on something important, realising why I was running to my mat. I counted on yoga to 'fix' my problem of stress. After the practice, I would feel amazing and attributed it to the yoga as opposed to the incredible system that we all have, which calms the stressful thinking on its own. Consequently, I became dependent on yoga to feel good.

What would happen on the days when I didn't go to yoga?

I felt awful because I had created an illusory dependency on it and needed a hit. I would beat myself up, feel guilty for not going and spend my time pining over the next session I could get to. It couldn't come quickly enough.

Unbeknownst to me, the feelings of 'good' and 'bad' were not coming from doing or not doing yoga. They were in fact coming from the gift of *thought in the moment*. When I understood this, it changed everything. From then on, I was able to enjoy yoga for what it was. I found that I felt good without needing to go because my experience of feeling good wasn't coming from the practice but from thought in the moment.

The challenge with 'prescribing' solutions to stress or unwanted feelings is that the solutions are unreliable as they don't consider that thoughts fluctuate from moment to moment. Sometimes you may enjoy a quiet mind during yoga practice and sometimes you won't. It's not the yoga that determines your state of mind as there is something deeper going on based on some fundamental principles of life.

The three principles of experiencing life

My understanding is that there is a spiritual truth universal to all of us, that is, that the way you experience life is via three principles: The Principles of Thought, Mind and Consciousness.

These three principles are constantly creating your reality whether you know it or not. It is the same for everyone.

The Principle of Thought

Simply put, the very fact that you can imagine, speak, touch and smell is a result of thought giving you the ability to do so. It's neutral, and all it does is give you the experience of what you put into it.

If I were to ask you to think of a pink elephant, the power of thought gives you the ability to conjure the image in your mind in the moment, just like a projector on a movie screen. We know via thought that we are thinking, and we are of course feeling. It's the very thing that allows you to experience a beautiful sunset, a caress, your favourite movie and the list goes on. Thought doesn't have the ability to discriminate between good and bad, positive or negative, high or low, beautiful or ugly. It just is.

The Principle of Mind

This is what some people refer to as universal intelligence – the energy that gives life to us and nature. It is the same energy that gives rise to creative ideas, solutions and realisations.

The Principle of Consciousness

As I already shared in Chapter 1, the principle of consciousness is our capacity to be aware. Consciousness gives life to the thoughts we have and animates them through our senses.

These three principles are like the law of gravity. You may not be able to see gravity; nevertheless, it is constant and everyone experiences it. If we know that these three principles exist, it helps to understand what creates our reality, which can bring huge relief. When you understand that what you perceive is fluid and isn't real, feelings that you experience as negative have less of a grip on you.

Your inbuilt self-correcting system

Have you ever noticed that when you are lost in stressful thinking, your mind can settle down on its own at some point, without needing to do anything? Just like the body heals on its own accord, the mind has the power to self-correct.

I see this in my son all the time. One moment he is in the middle of his own thought storm – where he starts to have more thoughts about a thought – and the next he calms down and brightens up like the sun coming through the clouds to warm the day. Just like storms and clouds, thoughts come and go. They are transient. There is nothing you need to do with them as the moment will always pass. Like a snow globe, when you shake it up all the bits create a mini storm inside the glass. But if you leave it and do nothing, it will settle. This is how it works for us too.

All feeling is neutral

There is nothing wrong with feeling what you feel. All too often I see my clients sitting in judgment on how they feel and say things like "I know I shouldn't feel angry but..." or "I know I shouldn't feel guilty but..." Who says you shouldn't feel what you feel? All feeling is neutral until the ego decides to judge it.

Why am I sharing this with you? Because if you think that it's not okay to feel bad then you may well want to avoid 'bad' feelings by fuelling unhelpful behaviours to avoid them (eating too much, drinking too much or working too much), denying them or letting thoughts judge you.

We all have days where we experience feelings of sadness, guilt and upset as it's all part of the human experience. But these so-called unwanted feelings are just as important as rain is to dry land. Just as plants need rain and sun to grow, you need the lows to appreciate the highs.

It is highly possible that the main reason you judge the feelings you experience is because sometime in your childhood you were told you were wrong to have them. You have some hidden layers of thought. A classic example is being told that good girls don't get angry. So when we get angry we feel guilty, suppress it or even avoid situations like confrontations because we don't want to feel what we feel. The challenge with this is that the more we make these feelings wrong, or want to do something about them, the longer we get stuck in them. Here's how the layers of thought can go:

 First layer of thought – I feel low

 Second layer of thought – I wish I didn't feel this way / I should know better

 Next layer of thought – I don't want to feel this / How do I get myself out of here?

Why do kids bounce back more quickly from the downs? Because they don't judge their feelings. They simply let the system do the work to bring them back to centre.

It's not about whether you go up and down – because you will. It's about how quickly you bounce back! Bouncing back more quickly involves doing nothing and allowing your internal system to do the work.

When I lived in Bali, I used to meditate in the mornings. One morning I was sitting cross legged by the pool when I felt a hot sting between my legs. My usual modus operandi would be to have a good scratch until it bled. But this time my inner voice told me to leave it alone to see what would happen. To my surprise, after a minute the itch had gone. Usually, I would search to ease the pain, making it worse and taking longer to heal – sometimes leaving a scar. But this time, no scar and a far quicker bounce back rate – because I did nothing!

Remember, feelings say nothing *about* you. They are only ever sharing what state of mind you are in. You may think feelings know that your circumstances exist, but they don't. They are simply sign posts, letting you know whether you are being present or not. It is useful to understand what feelings are sharing with you because it lessens their hold.

When you know you don't need to believe every thought you have, it means you can live your life with more peace.

Inherit to disinherit

Has it ever occurred to you that 'your' feelings are universal and that they don't belong to you? When I first had this realisation, it stunned me. I had erroneously believed that these feelings were my own and that what I felt was unique to me. Until I discovered otherwise. I now know that we all inherit feelings (thought patterns) from those around us.

When I was a teenager, I carried a deep sense of loneliness everywhere I went – like the cloud that follows Eeyore in *Winnie-the-Pooh*. I used to think it said something about how unpopular I was, and I would fill this feeling with relationships that were no good for me. I would phone different friends, spending hours chatting because I hated being on my own. As

I became more grounded (well-balanced), this feeling receded but never left completely, cropping up over time.

When I had Leo, that unwelcome feeling returned to accompany me into motherhood. I noticed it would be most present when Leo and I were alone together, when a pang of dread would spring out of nowhere and grip me. I was confused over what this feeling was saying and where it was coming from, so I avoided spending time alone with Leo. I would busy myself doing other things so that when I handed him over to my husband or the nanny, I wouldn't have to feel it. In short, my own misunderstanding stopped me from having the close and present relationship I wanted with my precious son.

When my husband and I separated, I knew I would now need to spend more time alone with Leo, which I found increasingly difficult as my loneliness intensified when we were together.

Then came the bombshell realisation: I had inherited this feeling from my mother.

It came during an intense period of loneliness when I had taken Leo to the playground to distract myself. As he clambered over the bright yellow and red climbing frame, I looked into the sky for a moment and heard the voice of truth within speak to me: *This feeling you are in is not yours: It belonged to your mum.*

In that moment, I started to cry with deep gratitude because I suddenly saw the truth. I had inherited my mum's experience of being a mother. She too had found it difficult to give me her focused attention. Peace filled me as I finally understood why my mother hadn't played with me all those years ago. I could see what it must have been like for her, and I felt a deep compassion for her.

While I still have moments when that feeling of loneliness returns, I am learning to connect and play freely with my son anyway. I have come to realise that I can do the very thing that needs doing regardless of how I feel, and so can you. One of the implications of seeing feelings for what they are is that you will be able to take them less seriously than you once did. The presence of these feelings will never stop, but they will have less of a hold on you.

What I take away from this is that the way you feel has nothing to do with your circumstances. It's an inside job and your self-correcting system settles you down every time. It's not something you need a prescription for.

Once you have the insight to see that your stress is not coming from anything other than thought, the implications on you and your life are empowering. As the content of thinking holds no power over you, you will change the way you understand yourself, just like I did.

What if stress is just reminding you that you are living in the misunderstanding of what creates your experience as opposed to saying anything about your circumstances? What would joy do? Some questions to ponder.

Let's recap and reflect

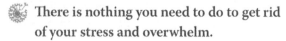 There is nothing you need to do to get rid of your stress and overwhelm.

It's through insight that effortless change occurs, which is something we are all built for. We each have a self-correcting system that brings us back to a state of clarity.

We perceive life through the principles of thought, mind and consciousness.

Stressful and overwhelming thinking is transient and will pass, just like the clouds.

Feel what you feel.

All feeling is neutral until you label it good or bad.

Judgments and analysis will keep you in the so-called 'bad' feelings longer.

It's not about whether you go up and down; it's about how quickly you bounce back.

Feelings don't know that your circumstances exist.

You can live a happy life irrespective of what you feel.

CHAPTER THREE

Finding the Joy in Others

*"Out beyond ideas of wrong doing and right doing
there is a field and I will meet you there."*

RUMI

Now that you have established where feelings come from and how your experience is created, I want to turn to how we can find joy in others – even in the most difficult relationships. My intention with this chapter is for you to see that you can create deeper connections with even the most 'difficult' people in your life, both professionally and personally – if you want to. It doesn't matter who the person is, the principles behind the Joy of Being play out the same.

Is there someone in your life who seems to drive you nuts? A family member, a member of your team or your kids?

Nine times out of 10 when I ask this question, there is always someone who comes to mind for that person. If you are currently experiencing difficulty with someone in your life, I hope that what I have come to understand about relationships will support you in navigating this area of your life with more ease and joy. I know my realisations have helped me enormously and I hope they will benefit you too.

Let's start with the most fundamental understanding of how relationships work – that of separate realities.

Separate realities

No two people live at the same level of consciousness or are experiencing life in the same way in any given moment. To assume this is possible creates an expectation, and, as with all expectations, it can create disappointment

At the talks and seminars I host, I often tell the story of Sherlock Holmes and Dr Watson as it points directly to what I am sharing here.

One day the famous sleuths decide to go camping. In the middle of the night Sherlock Holmes shakes his friend awake and clamours, "Dr Watson, what do you see?"

Watson looks up at the sky in awe. "Wow, I can see the Big Dipper, and if I look more closely I can see the Milky Way. Oh, wow, I just saw a shooting star! How amazing that you woke me up to see such a wondrous sight."

Dr Watson turns to Sherlock Holmes and asks, "What do you see?"

Sherlock replies, "Elementary, my dear Watson. Someone has stolen our tent!"

This is a classic example of two people experiencing the same thing from a completely different angle, illustrating how no two people experience life in the same way.

It's funny. I remember sitting with friends one evening and piping up with "Amsterdam has a lot of eye candy!" Everyone agreed apart from one person who asked, "What do you mean by eye candy?" I told him that I loved the buildings. The other two laughed as they realised their interpretation of eye candy was something completely different from mine! One of them said, "I thought you were talking about the men!" Someone else thought I was talking about the bicycles.

If you accept that we all live in separate realities, this can really help to lessen the expectation and disappointment that someone else has to behave in the same way as you. It also helps to respect someone else's point of view even if you don't agree with it. In fact, this understanding can encourage diversity and opens up an opportunity for deeper exploration and understanding. And remember, this book is all about how to have joy in simply being. By not placing as many unrealistic expectations on the relationships you have, it will help you to deepen and further your enjoyment of them.

It only takes one to change the relationship dynamic

In every relationship there is a dynamic. A dynamic is created by two people responding to each other in a particular way. If you find yourself in a challenging dynamic and want to change it, it's far easier to change the way you respond than expecting the other person to change. After all, you have no control over what anyone else does, no matter how hard you try! By changing your reaction, the dynamic must change.

When you are in a deadlock or having arguments, the best place to start is to notice where the ego is justifying its existence. It is easy for us to let the ego justify its reality, but it's best not to engage in another's drama – or ramp up your own. Remove yourself from the situation. Pause. Breathe. Not giving voice to that ego will bring you more joy in that area.

I am reminded of this quote by Victor Frankl:

> *"Between stimulus and response there is a space. In that space is our power to choose our response. In our response lies our growth and our freedom."*

But how do we go about not jumping to the bait when the reaction seems so innate?

To stay in the space, which I see as a type of inner stillness, it is wise to view everyone's behaviour as innocent, including your own. Remember, what you feel in the heat of the moment is giving rise to the power of thought in that moment. You will start to notice that as you experience more of this innate peace, you will react less often.

On a retreat in Lanzarote, Spain, I experienced a peace and stillness I had never felt before. At the time the relationship with my then-husband wasn't in a good place, and I found myself reacting a lot to his behaviour. On this day, he exhibited a behaviour that I thought was causing my distress. Instead of snapping at him and getting angry, however, I found a space that I hadn't experienced before, which helped me respond to him calmly. My usual modus operandi would have been to jump down his throat.

This one incident changed the dynamic. I realised that the stillness I was experiencing in that moment made space for a more helpful response. Everyone has knee-jerk reactions, but by experiencing peace more often, you will be able to shift the dynamic and exhibit a wiser response.

Not taking things personally – using discernment

When you feel someone is rejecting you, remember that their blame and anger has no power over you. The nature of thought is impersonal, and when someone gets lost in their personal thought storms, as we all do, it's innocent.

If this sounds like a riddle to you, let me share another story.

When Leo was five weeks old, I would get up in the middle of the night to change his nappy. Sometimes I would take too long to put his new one on and he'd pee or poo just after I'd cleaned him. On this occasion I was cleaning him up for the second time, wondering why I wasn't more annoyed, when it hit me: It was because I knew that Leo was totally innocent. He couldn't help it.

This brought to mind the endless arguments I'd had with people in my life, and I realised that we are all metaphorically pooing and peeing all over each other – which is innocent too. What I mean by innocent here is that they, you, we, fall back into the misunderstanding of how life works and think that our feelings come from the other person's behaviour.

Having insight to see the innocence in someone else's behaviour and our own makes for a more compassionate 'way of being' toward them and ourselves. As you see that no one can make you feel anything, and similarly that you cannot make someone feel something, you discover that you are not responsible for how people feel.

No one can hold any power over you – period.

This doesn't mean that you need to be okay with someone's rage, anger or manipulative ways. Neither does it give you free reign to be mean to others. It's okay to speak up and to share the fact that you are not okay with how someone behaves, if it makes sense for you to do so. It's healthy to voice what you want and what you prefer: We each live in separate realities. Doing so can deepen someone's understanding of you and you of them.

Consequently, there may be times when you find yourself saying goodbye to people around you who are not good for you. Rest safe in the knowledge that you deserve to be happy, just as they do.

I don't know about you, but over the last 20 years I have had to let go of a great number of friendships that were no longer serving me. What I took away from these experiences was the importance of having a strong connection and good communication skills.

Quality of connection and communication

Have you ever found yourself thinking of someone and suddenly they call you or you bump into them on the street? Or you feel so at one with someone else that you cannot distinguish where you end and where they begin? These are all examples of the capacity you have for connection.

Nevertheless, we can all experience disconnection in moments of anger, annoyance, rejection, hurt, upset or shutdown. In those instants, it may look as if you are separate from life, from the other person, but what has happened is that a thought storm has rolled in to cloud it. The quality of the connection at this point goes south while compassion, love and understanding disappear behind a cloud of insecurity.

The quality of your connection will always be determined by the Three Principles. The deeper the connection and the more presence of mind you bring to the moment, the better you will communicate. If we look at what communication is, we can see that it's comprised of two parts: expressing ourselves and listening.

Expressing ourselves

How we express or don't express ourselves is due to our state of mind. I used to think that there were certain things I couldn't talk to my ex-husband about, like money. There was a time when we started to use a joint credit card. That's when we had some of our most explosive, angry outbursts.

Let's just say there were some late payments, which affected my credit rating. My reaction was to get angry. The conversations I would have during a tantrum went something like this:

"How could you have dropped the ball?"

"Didn't you know that this was going to affect me?"

"How could you be so irresponsible?"

My anger would escalate, and I would shout at him for being so selfish.

This may seem like a reasonable reaction, but it was unhelpful. Once again I had been hijacked by angry feelings, thinking that my ex's behaviour was upsetting me. I would blame him, and he would argue back to protect his reality. Then it dawned on me that attempting to find a solution when we were both angry was not working. Our financial situation and his behaviour weren't the reason for our arguments. They were a consequence of our insecure thinking getting in the way of the connection, which then fuelled the spiral of negativity between us.

Interestingly enough, there were days when we could talk about our finances without getting upset at each other. When we didn't feel attacked, we were more likely to listen to one another and be open to what the other had to say without feeling the need to defend our point of view. This way we would be more likely to find a creative solution to our challenges.

Contrary to what most relationship experts think, our upsets were not being exacerbated or even caused by the content of our conversation, but rather the bad mood we were in.

Listening

Most of us don't listen to others properly because we are too distracted. Nevertheless, listening to someone with intent and giving them a hundred per cent of your attention brings presence to the moment. When you both listen deeply to one another, you are more likely to hear beyond what is being said. Listening with presence fuels compassion and understanding, and it is very rewarding.

In my bestselling book, *Goodbye Mr Ex*, I share a moment with an ex-boyfriend of mine who was so angry with me for how our relationship ended. My immediate response was to defend myself, but all of a sudden I heard "Shut the f*** up and listen!" As I stopped and listened more deeply, what I experienced was miraculous. I heard a small boy crying out for love. In that moment, all I felt was a huge amount of compassion for him.

When he finished sharing what he was feeling, I realised that all he wanted to do was to get the anger off his chest. Once there was no retaliation from me, the anger had nowhere else to go and before we knew it, we were back in a good feeling again.

I found myself saying to him, "That must have been so difficult for you".

To which he replied, "Yes, it was".

Even if the other person is caught up in a thought storm, it's possible for you to remain calm to increase your level of understanding and compassion.

Let's recap and reflect

 Insecurity is innocent and not personal.

 Behaviours are not an example of who we are. They illustrate habits of thinking.

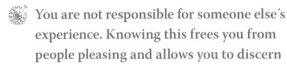 You are not responsible for someone else's experience. Knowing this frees you from people pleasing and allows you to discern who you want in your life.

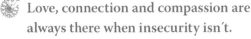 Love, connection and compassion are always there when insecurity isn't.

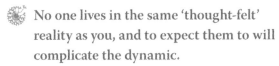 No one lives in the same 'thought-felt' reality as you, and to expect them to will complicate the dynamic.

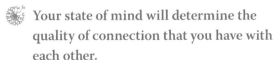 Your state of mind will determine the quality of connection that you have with each other.

CHAPTER FOUR

Breaking Away from the Money Trap

*"When we realise we don't need anything at all,
we are free to have it all."*

IAN WATSON

Just as relationships cannot give us a feeling, neither can money. When my clients insightfully see that money cannot give them a feeling of security, or any feeling for that matter, their emotional detachment helps them to experience more joy in this area of life. When they become less consumed by worry and fear, it makes way for more creative ideas on how to generate money and look after it.

Insecurities may well show up regardless of your own money circumstances as it's one of the most misunderstood resources that we have at our fingertips. Money is good for buying, spending and investing in assets, but it's dreadful at giving you a sense of wellbeing. It simply cannot do so. If you expect it to do something more, is there any wonder there is so much confusion.

If you innocently think, as I did for many years, that having money can give you a feeling of safety, of course you will associate money with a good feeling and will innocently believe that it's money you want more of.

The misunderstanding of where security comes from starts at a young age. My son has a security blanket called Budah (Bud-ah), which he uses to self-soothe. Perhaps as a child you had your own version of Budah and grew up thinking that an object could give you security. You may no longer need to sleep with a teddy to give you security, but money now has taken its place. Is there any wonder that 'financial security' is bandied around so much?

The challenge is that if you associate money with safety, you may live in fear of it disappearing, robbing you of the joy of what it can give you. The good news is that whatever your situation, money is not the culprit for any experience you have, as real as it may appear. It's just not true.

If you are reflecting at this point and challenging the notion that money cannot give you a feeling, consider this…

 Have you ever met someone who is rich and miserable?

 Have you ever met someone who is rich and happy?

 Have you ever met someone who is broke and miserable?

 Have you ever met someone who is broke and happy?

The chances are that you have.

Money neediness vs money need

Hardworking mums who experience money-related worries and struggles do not realise that it is related to their insecure thinking. If you think money gives you a feeling of security that may explain why you experience financial lack. Ironically, this simple and innocent misunderstanding is what keeps creating money effortlessly at bay. You end up being the puppet on the money string and dance to its tune as opposed to your own.

In one of my workshops that focuses on abundance, I talk about this neediness of money as if going on a needy date. Have you ever been on one of those? Or have you been the needy one? If so, you probably found the energy repelling. Money works in the same way: The more you are needy of it, the more it tends to stay away.

There is a distinction between money need and money neediness. We need money to live, and, if you run a business, to help it expand and grow. It's really useful as a tool to create experiences with and support you in creating the lifestyle you want. Money is just logistical – it's a tool. And just as we may need a hammer and nail to hang a picture on a wall, we also need money to stay in the game and play the game. We don't need to be needy of money but we can enjoy its uses, in the same way that we can enjoy a beautifully cooked meal.

Why money worries?

If you are wondering, *'How can I not worry about money? I'm a business owner! I am a hardworking mum with a pay cheque that could go at any moment. Of course I worry about it. It's part of being a hardworking mum!* ... well, here is the good news: Having a business or a wage and experiencing money worries don't need to go hand in hand.

You can experience peace by knowing that on the other side of worry is a solution – not just sometimes but always. When you are caught up in your money worries, it's often difficult to find a solution to the very thing you want to find an answer for. The solution is always there. The question is: Can you see it? The chances are that if you are stressed, it's going to be difficult to come up with something that can help you.

I remember when my former husband and I were at the train station in Madrid waiting for the fast train to Valencia. I was busy connecting with friends on Facebook and didn't realise the time. I heard a voice in the background say, "I'm going to the platform", and I mumbled a reply. A few minutes later I looked up and realised I only had five minutes to board the train. I ran to the entry gate but couldn't find my online ticket despite my panicked scrolling through emails. I called my husband to help, but he just looked disgruntled and upset because he could see what was about to happen.

By this point I was so stressed that I screeched at him to help. He kept saying, "Just look through your emails".

I couldn't find it.

In the end he went to Valencia without me as our son was waiting for us, and I was left crying with frustration because I had missed the train. As I sheepishly walked back to the ticket office and told them what had happened, they kindly gave me a new ticket at no extra cost. As my mind cleared and I calmed down, I made one more attempt at finding the ticket and suddenly there it was!

It had been in my emails the whole time.

I had been so stressed that I couldn't see the ticket. The solution was right in front of me, but my state of mind was so agitated that I couldn't see the solution! How often do we do that?

The solution is always there, but it's difficult to see when we are blinded and consumed by our thought storms.

Detachment leads to flow

Have you ever heard the saying that detachment leads to flow? If you haven't, or you have but are still confused by how to detach then what I am sharing with you here is the answer. When you realise that feelings of wellbeing don't come from money, you are free to live your life regardless of your financial situation. You are free to go with the ebbs and flows of the money river without it affecting you in the way it might be right now.

That's not to say that you don't need to manage it, nurture it or invest it. But it does free you up to be more in sync with it.

I pride myself on having some of the best mentors in the business, and what I have observed is the following: They enjoy their financial success because they are not attached to the money. They see it come and go and let it flow in and out without much thought. This is not to say that they don't manage and nurture it. They simply see money for what it is – a resource that supports their mission and lifestyle.

Tara's story

When Tara came to me, she was living in a constant state of worry about money. The experience she had of her business was one of stress and anxiety. She thought her worry was letting her know about her money and client situation, as opposed to her mood and state of mind. What she couldn't see was that her worry was an indication of how little clarity she had in this area of her life, as opposed to what was going to happen in the future and what had happened in the past. After having worked together for a couple of years, she has far less money worries and her experience of life is richer.

To give you a better understanding of her experience, I share here, with her permission, what she shared in my *Joy of Being* Facebook group.

Tara Mestre ▶ The Joy of Being: Unplug and Light Up

I had a bit of an incredible moment today. A client that had said they were going to resume work with me this month has decided to put it on hold. This time last year I would have taken it so personally and been so insecure that my services weren't good enough. I then would have worried about money and what this would mean for my finances. Instead I read the email and I heard that this client just didn't, for whatever reason, want to continue with her PR. I heard that this is a new opportunity for me work with a new client. I heard that my client is happy where they are at which is great. I heard nothing negative. I heard my wisdom telling me deep down that I didn't really want to work with them anyway because I didn't feel that aligned with them. Here's to hearing more and caring less!

What money loss taught me

Do you fear your money running out or not making enough of it? If so, you are not alone. Most of my clients feel the same way, as have I. Fear created the perfect environment for me to make investing decisions from a place of insecurity and greed. I invested in assets that I didn't understand and in other countries. After a couple of years, one of these investments stopped delivering and I lost half the money I had put in. The irony was that making a decision out of insecurity led me down the very path I wanted to avoid – the loss of my money. It taught me something invaluable about how we experience life.

When I heard that the oil well I had invested in would no longer produce, I went into a wild panic. Over the following months I would have acute moments of worry and upset followed by waves of peace. I realised that the future I had projected, about being devastated all the time, just wasn't true. I was experiencing all sorts of different emotions. There were days when I forgot what had happened and days when I would worry. These experiences were all transient – clouds passing through on a summer's day. I also got to see the truth that who I really am is okay with or without money. In other words, the loss of it couldn't damage or define me.

How much money you have or don't have in your bank account or business says nothing about who you really are. It reflects the thoughts and beliefs that you have about money – about generating, keeping and managing it. If you are not the car you drive, the house you live in or the holidays you take, how can you 'be' the money you have? It's just not possible.

What if the money story you have isn't even your own either?

Money stories don't belong to you

I used to think the movie I created about money was mine. But it wasn't.

In the middle of 2016, I noticed that I had an internal conflict around the money I had inherited. I knew it was something for me to enjoy, but I would break out into cold sweats when I spent it. I didn't believe it was mine to spend.

During my teenage years, I went to a privileged school but was bullied. It was during this time that I created a belief that rich people were mean and decided that I didn't want to have anything to do with them. Ironically, I was judging the very thing that I was – privileged and wealthy. So, I would hide and feel so ashamed of my background that I pretended to be poor.

As you can see, the gap between reality and me was quite wide, and I didn't know how to bridge it until a clarity bomb went off. The shame I felt was not mine: It was my father's.

I have memories of my mother and I wearing winter jackets in our home because my father worried about spending money on the heating, despite having thousands invested in the stock market. He would always send his letters second class and would even ask my mother to repay money she had borrowed to buy her own stamps. He would walk around with holes in his jumpers and wore the same jacket for about fifteen years.

An example of his own conflict arose one year when he invited me on holiday. I couldn't afford to go, so he told me he would pay and that I would be looked after. However, when it came to ask him for money to live on while I was there, he was angry and annoyed. He couldn't understand why I wasn't earning enough to fend for myself.

My dad thought his feelings were coming from the potential loss of his investments and money. This had a massive impact on me as I had been living out the same story – until I wasn't anymore because I insightfully saw what was happening. With this realisation, a huge weight was lifted. Ever since, I haven't felt guilty or had sweaty palms when I spend money.

We all live under the influence of others' stories and we recreate our own through our insights and revelations.

How much money you have or don't have reflects the thoughts and beliefs that you have about money.

Let's recap and reflect

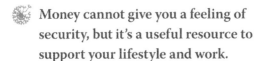 Money cannot give you a feeling of security, but it's a useful resource to support your lifestyle and work.

We need money to play the game, but we don't need to feel needy of it as there is more than enough.

When you are not attached to this resource and can see that it doesn't need to define you, you are free to have money and enjoy it.

You are okay with or without money as who you are has nothing to do with this resource.

Your net worth is no reflection on who you really are and what you are about.

Your money story doesn't belong to you: We inherit it from others.

PART TWO
LIVE MORE

*"Spend more time in joy and experience
more moments with presence."*

MARINA PEARSON

CHAPTER FIVE

Living from Wisdom

*"You only need to see one spiritual fact to change
your life forever."*

MICHAEL NEILL

Over the past chapters I have talked a lot about thought and consciousness and have only touched on the Principle of Mind. In this chapter I want to bring your attention to this principle because of its vital implication on understanding what is available to you and who you really are.

Mind is the spiritual energy of life itself and it is infinite. You may have heard it referred to as wisdom, creative ideas, uncontaminated thought, new thought, a shift in perception, an aha moment, a realisation, a voice, universal intelligence, a whisper, inner knowing, inner seeing, intuition, gut instinct, light bulb moment and so on. Suffice to say, it is the impersonal Mind where self-concern and judgment don't exist.

Discovering this spiritual fact has been a relief for me, and I hope it is for you too. You see, regardless of any insecurity you feel, this intelligence has the capacity to dissolve years of overthinking in an instant. Insecurity is an insight waiting to happen. This can happen when a new thought (insight) pops into your awareness, exposing you to the space within, to experience the stillness and joy you seek. It's an intelligent decluttering system that helps you empty your mind of all the piled up, unhelpful thoughts and beliefs that take up space. You don't need years of therapy because a new thought can help years of old thinking fall away in an instant.

Louise's story

When Louise and I started working together, she told me that she was still grieving her dad's death. During the five years after his passing, she had really struggled. She had attempted a number of avenues to get over what she was feeling, but his death still weighed heavy on her heart. She had been treated for depression and was wondering whether she would ever get over it. During this time, she became a mum but found it difficult to enjoy her experience of motherhood because of the depressive thinking she was still experiencing. She innocently thought that the reason she was feeling the way she was had something to do with her father's death, instead of her depressive thinking.

When we spoke on the phone, we talked about things unrelated to her so-called 'problem', when all of a sudden, she grew quiet and shared that all of her depressive thinking had dropped away in that instant.

A new thought had popped into her awareness and all the overthinking surrounding her father and her grief had fallen away. She later wrote that she felt light-hearted and the calmest she'd felt in years. Her outside situation hadn't changed – she was still sitting in the same café at the same table – but the experience of her father's passing had totally changed.

Wisdom is upstream

Wisdom is infinite, which means it will never run out. You are built for insight and will keep having aha moments for the rest of your life. Imagine a stream with an infinite source of clean water flowing into it, and the only way you can access it is by going upstream.

FORMLESS / UNIVERSAL / INFINITE
SPIRITUAL / FACT

I AM

THE SOURCE

↓ ↓ ↓ ↓ ↓

CLEAN

WORLD 2   **UPSTREAM**

FORM
AFTER THE FACT
BELIEFS
STORIES
CONSTRUCTS

DOWNSTREAM

CONTAMINATION

I first saw a version of this illustration in a book called *Clarity* by Jamie Smart.[1] As you can see from the picture, by going upstream you get in touch with the spiritual nature of who you are and the clarity that exists before contamination.

If you go downstream into the contaminated waters you are being exposed to the same habitual thought patterns, stories and beliefs. Finding clarity in the murkier waters would be impossible for most of us.

Clarity of mind comes from going upstream – looking inside and listening to your infinite source of wisdom. Some call it 'soul', 'inner voice' or intuition.

By Christos Georghiou

The test

If you are wondering if you have this super power, I invite you to look at the picture above.

---

[1] Smart, Jamie, *Clarity: Clear Mind, Better Performance, Bigger Results,* UK: Capstone (26 February 2013)

What do you see? Is it the tree? If so, can you see the faces? If you have just seen the faces then you have just had an insight. You went from not seeing what was right in front of you to seeing it with clarity.

I particularly like playing this game with the FEDEX logo. I invite you to bring up an image of the logo on your screen and look for the arrow and spoon that are hidden in it. When you see the symbols for the very first time, you know you have had an insight!

You are born with the capacity to have insights and will have them until the day you pass. How do I know? I invite you to go back to the moment you didn't know how to walk, talk or even crawl. When Leo was born, he wasn't able to do any of these things. But soon enough he started to take action on these things, and before we knew it, he had started to crawl, pull himself up and stagger from one sofa or table to another. Then one day he let go and took a step. Then he took another and another. All these stages were born of insight. You also learned to walk in the same way.

When does insight show up?

When you experience confusion, insight will come along and help you see through it. It shows up when it's good and ready. One moment we are walking around in one reality and then, in the next, an 'insight grenade' is thrown into our 'inside space' and we are in a whole new reality – one we didn't even know existed.

I will share a very personal story here that took place not long ago and involved a misunderstanding I had around intimacy. If I look back on my life and relationships, I can see how I pushed physical intimacy away because I thought it would hurt me. Let's just say my 'first time' was disappointing and I was deeply hurt. In that moment, unbeknownst to me, I had decided that having sex was too painful to have sober, and I would always have drunk sex. As I deepened my understanding of how life worked and began to experience more joy and peace of mind, I started to notice that my experience of sex was becoming one of more enjoyment. One day when I was reflecting on this, I realised that when I now had sex I was sober and that my need for alcohol had subsided.

Nevertheless, the act of exploring in the bedroom was still deeply uncomfortable for me until I had a powerful insight, which happened as my ex-husband and I decided to separate. The flash of insight came in the form of a deck of cards falling in on itself, and every card represented a past relationship. At the time I didn't understand what it meant, but when I was asked to explore in the bedroom, and I said yes without hesitation – and really enjoyed it! – I realised that all my old beliefs about sex, exploration and safety had fallen away. And in their place came joy and a new behaviour!

Listening to your wisdom/intuition

How often do we ignore our deeper, inner wisdom? How often do we distract ourselves by rushing around, not making time for the quiet reflection that helps us listen to what our soul/inner voice has to share? The voice of the clear waters of wisdom within.

I have found that wisdom can show up in different forms to tell us things: a yell, a soft whisper or a nudge, something you feel drawn to or something you get curious about.

Sometimes I ask my clients:

- **Where does the energy want to go?**
- **What are you being drawn to? (another way of asking the first question)**
- **What resonates for you?**
- **What is ringing true for you?**

You may have your own version of this same question. The fact is wisdom speaks to us in different ways. If we don't listen and continue to ignore it, the universe (wisdom) has a way of making us pay attention. Examples of this might include divorce, bankruptcy, business failing or illness. The signs are always there, but are we listening and paying attention?

Illness is a classic example of not
listening to our bodies.

I have found that when wisdom has nowhere else to go, it usually manifests itself in the body. I have been reminded of this again recently! Since my son was born, my energy levels have been yo-yoing. Any time Leo was ill, I would fall ill. In the last year I've had two bouts of food poisoning and I started to notice that I had bad body odour. At the beginning of the year, I got a chest infection, which was unlike me, and began to cough a lot. In short, my body needed attention and my immune system was compromised. To my mind, working was more important than looking after myself and I was busy, busy inside – which kept me busy, busy outside.

Finally, I listened to my intuition and just knew I had to stop working. I decided to take some time out of my business because I was completely exhausted. This gave me some space to listen more. As 'luck' would have it, I learned that some friends were in the area on a visit, and I invited them over for dinner. It turned out that they lived in Bali and he specialised in colonics and live blood analysis. My curiosity was piqued and knew I wanted to look him up on my planned trip. When I arrived in Bali, I sent him an email saying I wanted to have a colonic and an analysis. For some reason I had been afraid of doing one of these for years, but somehow that didn't matter anymore.

On the first visit, I remember thinking *Hey, I actually feel fine. What am I doing here?* But, as we dug more deeply and he did his thing, we discovered I had highly acidic blood and my large intestine was full of toxins. I needed a clear out. After a couple of treatments, I experienced what energy was supposed to feel like, and I realised that booking myself in for the detox retreat had been the best thing I could have done for myself.

Listening to what my body needed and taking action, I lost five centimetres of fat around my waist and my energy levels improved. Having realised the importance of listening to my intuition, I had trusted where my curiosity wanted to take me. I cannot encourage you enough to do the same.

The trust factor and making decisions

Trust what you hear within and what you are being drawn to and make your decisions from there. Yes, I know.... This can often be difficult for a lot of us: *How do I know whether what I hear is insight or insecurity?*

You will know because you will say things like, "It occurred to me" or "I suddenly came up with an idea" or "It just made sense".

The answers always lie upstream and not downstream in the contamination of your confusion or problems. When you relax, go about your day and trust the answer to arrive, insight will come out of nowhere as fresh, new thought. Sometimes it may even surprise you by prompting you in a direction or to make a decision that your ego was not expecting.

As a hardworking mum you make thousands of decisions every day, and I am sure you are making more wise decisions than you give yourself credit for. All too often mums tell me that they don't trust their wisdom, yet when they share their stories, I hear wise choices being made all the time. They just haven't recognised it. You are no exception. You too have common sense.

Noticing the wise decision

There are times when insight doesn't show up and you need to make a decision regardless. While you may not know whether that decision is the right course of action or not, you will be able to correct your course along the way. You can relax knowing that you couldn't have made another decision based on your level of awareness in that moment.

Here are some questions to ask yourself when you have to make a decision but no insight is showing up:

Where do I think feelings come from?

Do I think I am feeling my future or my past?

If I put my insecurity aside, what decision would I make?

If I know that my feeling of security and wellbeing lies within me, would I still be making this same decision or a different one?

If I know that there is no future or past, what decision would I make right now?

When you can make decisions based on now, not your past or future – and know that your security and wellbeing don't lie in the outcome – you are free to make decisions without fear or regret. Or without rushing into anything because you think time is running out. You can rest in the knowledge that insight will show you the way. Yes, you can worry and get upset, but it won't make insight show up any sooner!

Let's recap and reflect

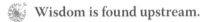 Wisdom is found upstream.

You are built for insight and innovation.

Insight shows up when it is good and ready.

Insecurity is an insight waiting to happen.

Decision-making is best made with clarity of mind.

Notice and follow the signs/breadcrumbs.

You don't need to take every thought you think seriously.

CHAPTER SIX

Re-discovering Your True Identity

"The real you is timeless before life and death."

SRI NISARGADATTA MAHARAJ

Now you know about wisdom and what it can do for you, let's move on to the subject of identity – who you are versus who you think you are. I have already pointed to the spiritual fact that you are the joy you seek, and that it exists inside. I have found this one truth to relieve a number of judgments, criticisms and limiting beliefs. Seeing beyond who you think you are to truly knowing whom you are is enormously helpful if you experience feelings of 'not enoughness'.

As you may have discovered, the quest to feel enough can be exhausting. It amazes me to meet smart women who on the outside appear to have it all and yet don't feel enough. Striving, people pleasing or over-spending to fill the illusive void are some ways in which the 'not enoughness' expresses itself. Enough!

The horizon effect

The quest for 'enoughness' fuels our need to strive. When we strive, what we are really saying is that we are not happy with where we are. If only we had arrived at our destination, we would feel better about ourselves. This then drives our need to always want more and gets in the way of us being content with what we already have. We pedal furiously toward an elusive future that doesn't exist. I call this 'the horizon effect'. When you look out to the horizon you can see it, but no matter how hard you attempt to reach it or touch it, it eludes you, just like a mirage in the desert – it's an illusion. There is nowhere you need to be, nowhere you have to get to: There is only ever now.

Like a hamster on a wheel, you go around and around, spinning the wheel faster, all in an attempt to arrive somewhere. But the destination is elusive and never arrives. You can always earn more money, work harder, strive for more... but when is enough enough? How will you know when you have arrived at the desired destination? The place where you feel the way you want and have achieved what you want?

This way of living is tiring and extremely dissatisfying. It is anything but joyful. Most of my clients use this strategy in an effort to avoid being alone with their insecure thoughts, which seem to get louder when they don't busy themselves with action.

What they have not considered is that the feeling of 'not enoughness' is not true, no matter how real it looks to them.

Years ago I decided to go on a retreat in Wales to press the pause button on my life. One day we were asked to sit in one of the many fields that surrounded the retreat and do nothing but notice what we could hear and see. I sat in the field, I looked around, I listened. Out of nowhere I heard a beautiful voice say, "If being is enough, you must be enough."

I know this message to be true by the very nature of what you are and what you are not. And what I can tell you is that you are not your body!

You are not your body

Have you ever considered that you are in fact not your body? If you haven't, consider this: *What if it is merely the vehicle we live in, to experience touch, smell, sight, pleasure, pain and so on?* If we are our bodies then why is it possible for them to change, morph and in some cases disappear when we find ourselves in the zone?

I had not considered this possibility until my father died.

My father passed away from pneumonia at Basingstoke Hospital in the UK in 2012. He was 92. I was very lucky to be by his side when he died. We had become close during the last years of his life, but it hadn't always been that way.

My father was an eccentric. He would sometimes show up at my school with his slippers and dressing gown on. And on one of those really lucky days, he would come to school without his teeth in! There was a large age gap between my mother and father, so when he turned up like this at school, I used to tell my friends he was my granddad because I was so embarrassed. There's nothing like your dad turning up to school without false teeth and with slippers to really ruin your street cred at the age of 11.

I guess as a little girl, I didn't understand how his upbringing had affected his capacity to interact with children and understand them. He had a harsh Victorian childhood, where children were seen and not heard, and his relationship with his own dad was a difficult one.

Bearing this in mind, he didn't really know how to be around a small girl, which is why we didn't have much of a relationship until I was able to understand why he had found it difficult to relate to me.

In 2008, when my first marriage ended, I went back to live in London and that's when my relationship with him changed. We began spending more time together, and I saw his personal struggles as just that – nothing to do with me. Understanding his conflicts with his father made it easier for me to put aside my judgments and see him for the wonderfully talented and witty human being he was.

When my sister phoned one morning to tell me Dad had been rushed to hospital, my first thought was that he would be fine. It wasn't the first time I would be visiting him in hospital, as I had done so many times before, and he had always bounced back. I wasn't too worried.

However, when I entered his room, what I experienced was very different from what I had imagined. The energy was frenetic with nurses bustling in every hour to check on my father. It was obvious the pneumonia had started to affect his cognition as he struggled to be coherent and would lapse in and out of recognising me. He grew confused about what he wanted – one moment he wanted food, the next he didn't. He wanted to leave and then he wanted to stay and rest.

This carried on until 7pm when everything went quiet and the nurses stopped coming into his room. He sat in a chair beside me while I laid on the bed, holding his hand as we watched the news together. At about 7.15 pm I felt his hand go weak. I turned towards him, saw that he had his eyes closed and thought he had fallen asleep. It then dawned on me that he had died. I jumped off the bed and ran out to get a nurse. Despite the context, it was a beautiful moment I will treasure forever.

As my father was carried to another room, I was given some time to decide whether I wanted to go in and see him. I resisted for a moment, uncertain. Nevertheless, I walked into the room to see him one last time. I'm glad

I did because it gave me further insight into who we are and what we are made of.

As I walked into the room where he lay, I was surprised to find that he didn't look like my dad at all. He looked fifty years younger. He looked translucent and at peace. All his frown lines had disappeared completely. That is when the realisation hit me: *Who he was wasn't his body*. If that had been the case, he wouldn't have looked so different. It then struck me that this process is the same for all of us when we pass on. Life leaves and all that is left is the body.

You are not the thoughts you have

What would happen if one day you discovered that who you thought you were was all made up? What if you were to learn that you are so much more than you think you are? I remember one of my friends asking me, "Who is the 'I' that you refer to on a daily basis?" This stopped me in my tracks as I had always assumed that the 'I' I talk about is me, Marina – a woman, joy coach, the *Joy of Being* podcast host, divorcee, mum, investor, bilingual in Spanish and who lives in Javea, Spain. While all of that is true, these are nothing more than labels I have given myself. Over time I have come to see that I don't know who I am. It changes from moment to moment based on thought. As it does for you.

For many years, I had bought into the notion of 'who I am' as being a fixed thing. I am Marina, who is this way. I totally believed the bull crap I would say to myself about who I thought I was, and it didn't look pretty – especially during my teenage years. By the time I was 13 or 14, I believed all the bad things I would say about myself. I am fat, ugly, stupid, unpopular (and so the list went on).

In an effort to silence the critical voice, I decided to stop eating and slowly anorexia took hold and sucked me in. I became obsessed with how much control I had over my body and how little I could put in my mouth. I believed that if I were beautiful and thin enough, I would be lovable.

These patterns of thinking accompanied me throughout my twenties and most of my thirties until I was pregnant and had profound insights into who we are. During the first three months of my pregnancy, I spent a lot of time in bed because I was so tired. One night as I was lying there alone, the question *Who am I?* popped into my awareness. I didn't really know how to answer that, so I didn't. A few seconds later I heard 'I am...' I waited a little longer to find out 'what', but there was only silence.

I AM.

We are not what we label ourselves. We are not the roles we play, the jobs we have or the results we get. They are what we do, not what we are.

You are not your roles or feelings

We are capable of giving ourselves labels and roles, but they don't need to define us. I haven't always seen it this way. I used to think that my identity had something to do with the roles I played. That meant that each role had a story attached to it, which I very much identified with.

I work with a lot of mothers in business who innocently mistake their different roles for who they are. They may wear many different hats – mum, business owner, wife, sibling or divorcee – and each role has its meaning. It's so easy for us to fall into this trap from time to time. After all, when asked what you do, we usually reply with "I am…" as opposed to "I do… (this or that)".

When I work with clients who are in their own identity trap, I show them the following model, which opens their eyes to a new way of seeing themselves:

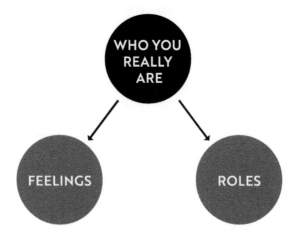

The basic premise of this little diagram is that you are not the feelings you have nor your roles that you play out. Let's start with the *feelings* part. Have you ever said to yourself any of the following?

 I am tired.

I am overwhelmed.

I am sad.

I am depressed.

Well, any of these labels can be introduced with a feeling in front of them:

I am (feeling) tired.

I am (feeling) overwhelmed.

I am (feeling) sad.

I am (feeling) depressed.

The cool thing about the way we feel is that it is transitory and comes and goes in the same manner as our thinking. This is because feeling and thinking are different sides of the same coin. So we cannot 'be' our feelings as they come and go.

Our roles are similar.

I used to see my roles as 'who' I was, especially the work role. When I moved to New York in 2005 to join my first fiancé, my identity was so wrapped up in my work that I thought I *was* my job. Before leaving my employment in Madrid, Spain, I was given the role of Export Manager at a record label. This meant I was the face of their international department, and I was responsible for organising the fun events at MIDEM and Popkomm, the two most important international music industry events of the year. It was an enormous responsibility ensuring the international department grew and progressed. The job challenged me, just the way I liked it.

However, when I got to New York, I was met with a very different scenario. As part of my master's in Music Business, I had to work as an intern. I made coffees and did plenty of tedious administrative tasks, none of which I found challenging in any way.

Because my identity was so wrapped up in my work and its associated job labels, I soon felt depressed and lost. I thought that my self-esteem had come from my label of Export Manager, and that without it I was worth nothing. As time passed, I realised that I didn't want to work for anyone else and I wanted to help other people. I decided to become a coach and help others change their lives. However, striving to make the business work would inevitably get in the way of enjoying the journey. When I gained recognition from different publications and the media for my book, I felt successful. But when I wasn't getting that attention, I felt unworthy and empty.

Yet I have found that there is something that is constant. Some call it essence, life force, spirit, or soul. Words can't do it justice. All I can say is that your state of being is very quiet as you fall back into the present moment. Some refer to this as a sense of 'coming home'. I call it 'sitting in your true being'. I realise now that when you bring presence to the moment and the world stops, there is nothing you need. You already have everything you could possibly want.

If you are reading this and thinking, *I have never experienced that before*, let me share that you probably have. You just may not have realised it. Having had insights, you will have experienced stillness. Therein lie the answers you and I look for.

Even though I have experienced it, I doubt I will ever discover what that essence truly is. And that's okay. That's part of the mystery, and that leads me to my next insight.

What pregnancy taught me about who we are

The next insight I had about our true nature came when I was walking the streets of London, three months pregnant with Leo. As I walked a new thought popped into my awareness. *What is growing Leo?* I knew I wasn't. After all, I didn't have to think him into existence, and I didn't need to do anything actively. A natural process was taking care of that.

Then I grew curious about what was creating him. What was giving him a nose, an eye, a mouth, a liver? What was creating this incredible organism? And then it hit me... OMG, it's the same intelligence that created the sun, the mountains, the sea and all that we experience in nature. It's the universal intelligence that gives life to everything. Call it GOD (Grand Orderly Design), love or the Universe. Whatever you like to call it, it's what you are. You are not separate from life, even though sometimes it may feel that way. At one point you were formless, an idea which was brought into being to experience life on Earth.

Finally, I understood: We are all one and separation is an illusion.

Tears started to run down my face in awe of this magic, of this truth, of the grand design that unifies us all. And in that moment I felt at one with everything around me. I saw how we are all one. The universal energy creates everything – no exceptions. Life is life-ing and your body is a conduit for it. You are so much more than you think, which means you are more than enough.

Let's recap and reflect

- Even if you don't feel enough, you are enough.

- Your true nature is before form and infinite.

- You are not your body, insecure thoughts, unhelpful behaviours or roles – YOU ARE.

- There is nothing you need that you don't already have.

- You are born of the universal intelligence that created everything.

- You are not separate from life: You are life.

CHAPTER SEVEN

Innate Confidence

"What lies behind us and what lies before us are tiny matters compared to what lies within."

RALPH WALDO EMERSON

Are there areas in your life where you experience more joy, confidence and success? Are there other areas where you feel stuck and wonder why you can't get a grip on things? Every mum I have ever worked with always has areas where she excels and areas where she feels hindered. You may well be wondering what is going on, and I wanted to use this chapter to support you in deepening your understanding, to give you more clarity in the areas that you don't feel exist for you.

What area of your life do you experience confidence in, where it is easy to spend time? Is it your work or your health? Do you struggle in the area of your kids or intimate relationships? A trend I see in most clients is that they are amazing at their work but don't see the area of their health or personal relationships as clearly.

The simple reason is this: *Where you have clarity of mind you will excel, and where you have a high level of insecurity you won't, or you won't excel as much!*

When you have a lot on your mind, it's difficult to navigate with ease in that area. But when you have nothing on your mind you will experience joy and know exactly how to take what you do forward. It's a simple equation really, which I call *The Confidence Equation.*

Lots on your mind = Insecurity
Nothing on your mind = Confidence/Joy

The key to getting clarity of mind around the various areas of your life is to understand your 'Zones of Ease' and your 'Areas of Resistance'.

Areas of ease vs resistance

Just as you will have parts of life where you struggle, you will have areas where you excel because they are your zones of ease. A zone of ease can be described as a zone where you see what others don't, where you are totally aligned with how life works and therefore you are grounded in reality more of the time.

You may have spent time with your craft, and now, with years of experience, it has become easy. Maybe you had a knack from the outset. Some of my clients have service-based businesses that were born from something they felt passionate about and that they were really good at. The value they bring to their clients is the peace of mind they have in the area that their clients don´t. I know that my clients will eventually learn profound lessons from their journey and become better at certain aspects of their work and life. The more peace of mind you have in general, the easier it is to learn to do things anyway.

Explore the areas you are resisting

How do you gain more clarity in the areas that you resist and, in turn, experience success and joy in them? The answer is really simple: *Explore them!*

You may have been caught up in the 'I'm not ready' trap, but you know what? You don't need to feel ready to start. Take the first step just as you did as a baby, and the action you take will help you gain more insight into the area of exploration. Something that has been difficult once can become easy if you explore it. Let me give you an example.

For the longest time I knew that I wasn't managing my money well, but I didn't want to look. I resisted looking, and every time I thought about doing so, I would hear the same story: "This money stuff is too hard, and I am just not ready to look".

In the end I couldn't ignore what I was manifesting any more. In August 2016 it came to the point where I had to sell assets to make it through the month. My cash flow had dried up as I was waiting for a property to sell. My money was all tied up and I had to sell the last of my gold at a loss.

Around this time I received an email about a course run by my incredible mentor Ann Wilson, the Wealth Chef. As I watched the first three free videos in the series, it became apparent that I needed to take responsibility for how I managed my money. The irony of this was that I had to get an overdraft to pay for the course.

As I dove in and made it my priority to never find myself in the same situation again, I started to have insight after insight into money management. At the beginning it was tough going as I had a lot of insecure thoughts. It was a steep learning curve as I had to learn about balance sheets, income statements and stocks. As I put in the work, over time it became easier and easier. Now my relationship with money management is better aligned with reality and how it works compared to the way it used to be. I see this area of my life with much more clarity, and therefore I can handle it with more confidence and less resistance.

Yes, I can always explore more and see more in this area, but I realised there was nothing to be afraid of. The resistance I had initially felt was not letting me know about money management, but rather about thought in that moment. This experience taught me that when we take action, regardless of how we feel, we will have insights along the way to clear the path. The great news is that each insight ripples out peace to other areas of your life too.

Morena's story

Morena was a client who joined my Effortless Business Program that helps women in business achieve a more peaceful and therefore effortless experience of their business and life. She runs a bookkeeping business and was struggling to fill her practice while feeling guilty that all she did when she got home at night was work. She hated her corporate job and wanted to leave as soon as possible. We never discussed her corporate job, instead focusing on filling her practice. As time went by her need to have a fully functioning business fell away, as did the insecure feelings around her corporate job. She is now fully booked in her business and she loves her employment. I have seen this with countless clients: They get clarity on a specific area of life and this ripples out to other areas that we didn't focus on.

Confidence vs arrogance

Quite a few of my clients question the difference between confidence and arrogance. This confusion can often lead them to shy away from confidence because they don't want to be arrogant. But there is a clear difference between the two. Confidence is our true nature. Confidence is not concerned with personal gain or being better than the rest. It is fuelled by a willingness to serve when you have clarity of mind.

Arrogance is the opposite. Arrogance is fuelled by the little mind (some know this as the ego) and creates an image of self-importance. Arrogance is a strategy to protect us from vulnerability. It thinks that it is better than others and that we have something to prove. Arrogance is about being right and not caring about others nor wanting to understand another person's point of view.

If you care about what others think and this hinders you in some way, just remember that just because someone has an opinion doesn't mean it's true. Everyone paints their life via thought, and if they are lost in their own judgment of you, that is all that is going on. You may have misunderstood this in the past and taken what they think of you personally, but you don't need to. What's important is what you think of you. Even then, if you struggle with self-doubt and criticism, you can take action regardless.

A few years ago my ex-husband told me of a relationship conference that was taking place in London and asked me whether it was something I should be part of it. When I took a closer look, my arrogance took over and I told him that as I had not been invited to speak, I wouldn't do it even though there were opportunities to sponsor the event. A few weeks passed and he asked me whether I would change my mind. In that moment, I saw how arrogant I had been. I decided to look into sponsorship opportunities and gave the organiser a ring. We had a chat and I decided to go ahead and sponsor the event.

As we were talking, I asked if he would be open to me speaking for longer than the five minutes allocated for sponsors, and he agreed. While we were discussing this, a new thought crossed my mind. *Why don't you let him know you'd be willing to take a speaking slot if anyone else dropped out?*

Suddenly the judgments drowned out this new idea. *You can't do that, how rude!* So I didn't ask.

The day came, and as I was setting up, one of the speakers dropped out due to illness and the organiser suggested extending everyone's speaking time. In that moment I seized the opportunity and asked if I could take their slot.

And his answer was, "Sure, sorry I didn't think of asking you. It hadn't occurred to me". So not only did I get to promote my services and relationship event, *Your Pathway to Love*, I also got to speak for 20 minutes. Because of this opportunity I ended up with a couple of new clients and a number of attendees for my event.

> *Where are you not asking for what you want out of fear of rejection? What new opportunities could you create for your business and at work if you were to ask?*

Comparison and where your power really lies

When we compare ourselves to others, it's challenging to be joyful as judgment takes over. I used to spend so much time looking at where others were on their journey, how far they had gone, and evaluating that against how little I had seemingly achieved. One day when I was caught up in comparing myself to another coach, an insight came to me: *I want to feel how they look!* I thought that if I could be where they were, I would feel just as amazing as they looked on Facebook! And of course, this isn't possible.

If you experience this too, I invite you to stay in your own lane and focus on what you are up to. That's what I decided to do. Everyone has a unique path to follow, as do you. We are all having insights in our own time. Therefore, the way we live our lives and express our work will be different for all of us. Would you hurry and compare so much if you knew that there is nothing you need that you don't already have? When you spend more time in the 'being' state, you will notice how the comparisons fall away and you are less concerned with the competition.

We all have the capacity for insight, which means that *the real power lies within us.* I didn't know this a number of years ago and, looking back, I can see how that played out. I hired a lot of consultants and coaches because I thought they had the answers I was seeking. It was shortly after I had been introduced to the principles behind life that I had a major insight into this very thing.

When you spend more time in the 'being'
state, comparisons fall away.

I was at an experiential course where you play games and learn as you go, and I had been asked to be a team leader for one of the games. In truth, I didn't understand the rules and, as the game started, I thought I had better unite with another team as they would know what they were doing! When another team leader suggested we join forces, I was relieved. I made the assumption (as I had with most of my mentors) that they knew better than I did.

Within five minutes of joining forces, he took control. Two of my team asked me, "Why have you sold us out? Why is he running the team and not listening to you? He doesn't seem to know what he's doing".

As I thought about what they said, I realised that every time I didn't know what I was doing, I would give my power away to someone else and let them take responsibility. In addition, I saw how I'd made an erroneous assumption that everyone knew what they were doing when they were making it up on the spot, just as I was.

So please, remember. Know that your real power lies within you, and don't assume everyone knows better than you. Because they don't. Find your zones of ease but do explore your areas of resistance. By connecting to your inner voice and seeing that confidence is innate, you can excel in those areas too.

Let's recap and reflect

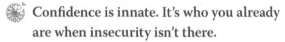 Confidence is innate. It's who you already are when insecurity isn't there.

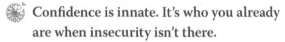 You will have areas where you will excel and where you won't, depending on your level of insecurity in each area.

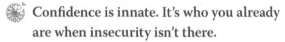 Clarity of mind matters as it allows you to see opportunities where you may have missed them under a shroud of insecurity.

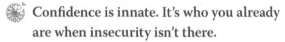 You can gain confidence in weak areas by taking action. Action leads to insight.

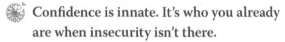 Resistance is an invitation to expansion.

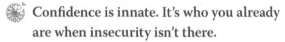 Comparing yourself innocently to others isn't where the answer lies: The power lies within you.

CHAPTER EIGHT

Falling in Love with the Unknown

"Life isn't about waiting for the storm to pass.
It's about dancing in the rain."

VIVIAN GREENE

As mums, it's easy for us to want to control all aspects of our lives: the kids, those closest to us or the outcomes of our work. You may think that controlling your outcomes or other people will help you avoid discomfort of the unknown. Control can come in many different guises: over-planning, not letting others help, manipulation, micromanaging, to name a few. Looking for security in these behaviours is not only impossible but also exhausting.

You cannot avoid unknowns and uncertainty. Life is a contact sport and you will experience (if you haven't already) situations that you were not expecting. Accepting uncertainty and change can help to weather the storms in times of difficulty.

Two worlds co-existing

Something that has helped me to move through times of uncertainty with grace is to know that we are spiritual beings having a human experience. You and I are operating in two worlds every day – the spiritual world and human world – but some of us may be experiencing one world more than other.

The spiritual world:
Where We Come From / The World of the Formless

The spiritual world is what we are born from, and the insights we have are a glimpse of this world. We all navigate life with more ease when we spend more time living from this place. It's our true nature.

When you operate from this world more of the time, your quality of life goes up. You are in the present moment more often and are less affected by the rollercoaster of thinking. Clarity, wisdom and peace reign in this world, which makes dealing with challenges and problems far easier. When we are home, quiet and in a beautiful feeling, it's a tangible experience of this world.

The human world:
Material World / The World of Form / After the Fact and Tangible

This is the world we were born into. This world exists as a result of the spiritual world. When you spend more of your time in this world, you tend to find yourself being gripped by thinking more of the time.

Can you relate to living in one world more of the time than the other? If it's the human world, keep looking in this direction and you will start to have a preference for the spiritual over the human world. And why wouldn't you? If navigating the unknown becomes easier then of course it makes sense. Understanding that you have been guided all your life by the innate intelligence you are made from enables your personal mind to relax. When this happens, the innate wisdom that runs through you will do the heavy lifting. Some have come to call this 'letting go'.

Universal re-arrangement: The art of letting go(d)

Not long ago I realised that letting GO(D) is a much more practical way of experiencing the 'dark' moments. And if you are wondering why GO(D) rather than *let go*, read on.

Remember, I shared with you back in Chapter 6 the insight I had about the Grand Orderly Design (GOD) creating everything and that we all come from that one energy? Well, if there is a grand order to everything, then the Grand Orderly Design must be guiding you and taking care of you even in times of change and perceptive uncertainty. You may not like the re-arrangement of circumstances especially prepared by the universe, but you can trust it.

How do you let GO(D) when your inner control freak is crying out for safety and order in moments of overwhelm and pain? As I embarked on a quest to heal my pain, I would often hear the trainer at the front of the seminar room say, "Let go!" and I thought *Well, how the hell do I do that?* I couldn't figure out how it was possible to let go of the outcome and attachment.

Then I came across the understanding that I share with you in this book. If I know nothing on the outside can cause me pain, worry, anxiety or fear – if I know these experiences are fleeting, as is thought – then I can simply detach from the outcome and let GO(D) do its thing, right?

You cannot trust your insecure, personal mind (ego) to see the bigger picture. This is because the ego clings to negativity, analysis and judgments for dear life. However, you can trust the universal intelligence of life, and the process. Just because you cannot see the bigger picture doesn't mean there isn't one. If you look back at your life, have you noticed how certain circumstances you saw as tragic turned out to be a blessing?

Detach from the outcome and let
GO(D) do its thing.

The ancient story of the Chinese farmer illustrates this point.

Once there was a Chinese farmer who worked his poor farm together with his son and their horse. When the horse ran off one day, neighbours came to say, "How unfortunate for you!"

The farmer replied, "Maybe yes, maybe no".

When the horse returned, followed by a herd of wild horses, the neighbours gathered around and exclaimed, "What good luck for you!"

The farmer stayed calm and replied, "Maybe yes, maybe no".

While taming one of the wild horses, the farmer's son fell and broke his leg. He had to rest up and couldn't help with the farm chores. "How sad for you," the neighbours cried.

"Maybe yes, maybe no," said the farmer.

Shortly thereafter, a neighbouring army threatened the farmer's village. All the young men in the village were drafted to fight the invaders. Many died. But the farmer's son had been left out of the fighting because of his broken leg. People said to the farmer, "What a good thing your son couldn't fight!"

"Maybe yes, maybe no," was all the farmer said.

~Anon

What I took from this story is that whatever happens to you just happens. It's the personal mind that interprets whether it's good or bad. Interpretations and fearful storytelling are something that we all do. Nevertheless, if you don't see fear for what it is, it can really hold you back from joy and freedom.

Beyond fear to freedom

Did you know that babies are only born with two fears: the fear of falling and the fear of loud noises? This means any other fears we experience in life are made up.

When fear is misunderstood, it can stop you from getting on with the action you need to take.[2] From the conversations I've had with clients, and from my own experience, the only way to move through fear is to take action on the very thing you think you are afraid of.

However, the thing you fear is not actually the thing you are scared of. Rather, it is the feelings that will arise within you that you are fearful of. Time and again I have been surprised by the way I react when faced with having to do something that scares me.

Four years ago, I was sitting in a seminar where the trainer wanted to demonstrate what the power of thought can do if we believe what we think. He described an exercise he'd taken part in where he was asked to go

[2] Listen to episodes 19 and 21 of my *Joy of Being* podcast where we explore the subject of *fear* with my guests; www.MarinaPearson.com/podcast

into a shop that didn't sell pizza and ask for a slice. We all giggled at the thought of him wandering into a store to order a pizza knowing that they didn't sell food. As he came to the end of the story, he shared that during the lunch break we would need to do the same exercise. My reaction to his suggestion was immediate! As I conjured up a fearful future of shop owners laughing me out the door, my palms started to sweat.

We discovered that each of us had experienced something similar. While we listened to his invitation, we had all conjured a vivid picture of this made-up future that looked terrifying and real to us, even though we hadn't left our seats.

As we broke for lunch, he asked whether anyone would do the exercise. Not surprisingly there were very few takers! In the end, I did go into a few stores to ask for pizza. I had a great time. It didn't feel the way I thought it would. In fact, all the people I asked were helpful and directed me to the pizza restaurant down the road.

The lesson here is that we never know how we will feel, and the feeling of fear says nothing about how it will turn out. The future is an incomplete equation that doesn't even exist. The future, like the past, is formed by the mind.

Leaps of faith

Knowing that the future is an incomplete equation can make taking leaps of faith much easier. Jumping into the unknown is not only about where you end up but also what you learn and who you become along the way.

Sometimes we need a reminder of the leaps of faith we've already taken in life when faced with a new one, like Tara, a client of mine.

Tara's story

Tara decided she wanted to leave her partner, and after much indecision she did. On one of our calls, she said she was having a really bad time because of all the changes. She had moved back to Ireland to live with her parents, wanted to make a career change and had not found a school for her son.

During our conversation, I mentioned that she must have taken leaps of faith before but had merely forgotten. I asked her to write down moments in the past where she had jumped into the unknown, to remind herself that what she was doing was nothing new. The following month we spoke again, and she told me how everything had started to fall into place. Her son was in a good school and she was making the career change to teach yoga, something she had always wanted to do. The relationship with her ex was also on fairly good terms.

She said writing the list had made her realise how many leaps of faith she'd taken in her life. She also recognised that whenever she had, things had fallen into place.

Sometimes you've got to press the 'f**** it' button (as I call it) and jump into the unknown to see what happens next.

The unfolding

Nothing ever remains the same. In nature plants grow and die with the beat of the seasonal cycle; the same is true for you. You are built for change just as you are built for insight. You may experience times of uncertainty where you are flung into the unknown, yet it would seem that the unknown is nothing to be afraid of. In fact, the unknown is where the magic happens.

Why? Well, you have no frame of reference for the unknown. In the same way as you entered motherhood, started your business or a new job, you began with a blank slate, discovering that you would learn as you journeyed on.

Life unfolds, which means you don't know exactly where you will end up or what the outcomes will be. Follow the breadcrumbs (wisdom's nudges, signs, whispers and so on) and this will pave your path. All you can do is take one step at a time just as you did when you learned to walk.

You see, you have no idea what lies in the future even though your mind attempts to figure it out. One of the things human beings are really bad at is predicting the unpredictable. No matter how many scenarios you have in mind, and no matter how certain you are of what you conjure up, the future is an incomplete equation. You will have not taken into consideration the insights, people and circumstances that will appear along the way to help and guide you.

Joining the dots

If there is any doubt that you have been guided on your journey of business or life, I invite you to join me in a game. I run an event called *Your Pathway to Effortless Business* where I ask the attendees to look at a result they created in their lives. I then ask them to look back at the events leading up to the result. The intention of the exercise is to give you insight into the guidance you receive and magic that exists each step of the way to create specific results, moments or experiences in life.

Here is an example of mine:

The Result: Signed up a client to my program

- A number of new people joined my database (because)...
- I said yes to being part of an online summit (because)....
- The organiser wanted me to be part of it. I knew her (because)...
- We met in Bali and had coffee together as she wanted to speak to me about her divorce (because)...
- A friend had introduced me to her...

As you can see by my example above, you can keep joining the dots *ad infinitum*. But this should give you clarity on how it works.

You will have your own version. So go ahead:

Write the outcome of something that is memorable to you.

 Write down the action that you took before it, and before that.

 Keep repeating this until you get to see that, yes, there is guidance.

If you are dancing in the uncertainty of the unknown right now and find yourself doing so in the future, relax. It always works out in the end.

Let's recap and reflect

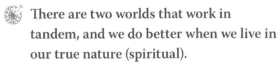 There are two worlds that work in tandem, and we do better when we live in our true nature (spiritual).

As you deepen your understanding of how life works, you will inevitably acquire a preference for living in the spiritual world more of the time.

Universal re-arrangement is inevitable, so let GO(D).

Good and bad is contextual.

The answer to any unknown is hidden in insight.

You are always being guided from moment to moment.

Jump and the net will appear as things have a way of working out.

CHAPTER NINE

The Art of Effortless Results

*"Your understanding of how life works has
more influence than any other factor over your
experience of life and the results you get."*

JAMIE SMART

Over the past chapters I have talked a lot about your spiritual nature and what is available to you with a quiet mind. Now I want to share how living from this place can support you to achieve the results you want without compromising your joy or energy. Most of the working mums I speak to are totally frazzled because the only way they have been taught to achieve is through *pushing*, *hustling* and *striving*. This feels like a hard slog, and in some cases it is taking them down the road to burnout. If there is a result you want to create, it's possible to achieve without running yourself into the ground.

The effortless results equation

We are built for results. This is the insight I had when I finished reading *Results* by Jamie Smart. As

I contemplated this insight, it dawned on me that of course this is true. If everyone is built for insight, you must also be built for results as insight is a major component in creating the clarity you need to move forward with any of the projects you have.

Clarity + Action = Effortless Results

When the mind is still generating, a result is far more fun and easier to execute. It's simpler to see what you need to do and how you need to do it if you have clarity of mind. As you become calmer and more joyful, people seem to be unconsciously drawn to the feeling you are in.

Ella's story

When I first met Ella her entertainment business was running her. She was at the beck and call of her clients and was taking care of tasks in the business that she didn't like and were not focused on her strengths. She hated the journey and felt she was being run ragged. She joined my Effortless Business Program because she wanted to work her business with more ease. One of her heartfelt desires that she got clarity on was to land corporate clients. On one of our calls five months in, she gushed with the news that she had effortlessly attracted Ascot Racecourse as a client because she had been recommended by another client who she had done amazing work for. She told us that she hadn't chased or even presented herself to them. But her previous actions in doing fantastic work for the client brought in her results.

The feeling you are in makes a huge difference to who you are being, and the actions you take with it are like rocket fuel. This results in people and prospective clients wanting to hang out with you, which in turn can generate more money with less effort!

However, the opposite can be true for anyone.

Stress + Action = Hard Slog

What gets in the way of creating a result effortlessly is insecure thought, which gets in the way of clarity. When your mind is full of noise – stories or judgments that you believe to be true – it makes it difficult to see the wood for the trees; hence the saying!

Do you need to wait until you have an insight? No, you don't. You can take action regardless of how you feel and learn along the way. Nevertheless, taking action when your mind is clear will give you a more joyful experience of the journey.

Toxic goals vs heartfelt intentions

There is a lot of controversy in the personal development industry as to whether you should set goals or not. My take on it is this: Set them if you want to. There is nothing wrong with creating them, unless you think that the goals you set will make you happy. There is a big difference between setting a toxic goal and what I call a heartfelt intention.

A toxic goal is an outcome that you think will give you a feeling of happiness or joy. It goes something like this:

Once I have x amount in the bank, I can be happy.

 Once I am successful, I can be happy.

 Once I go on holiday, I can be happy.

Any time you think that an outcome or a goal can make you happy, you have fallen back into the misunderstanding. The challenge with thinking that your happiness and wellbeing is dependent on reaching a goal is that if you don't attain it, you will struggle to find the joy you seek. Looking for happiness in goals is like looking for joy in the wrong place.

Nonetheless, if you do reach a goal and don't experience the feeling you expected, you may search for it elsewhere or think that you set the wrong goal. This misunderstanding will keep you striving and pushing for the security you seek, which cannot be found in the outcomes you create.

On the other hand, a heartfelt intention is an outcome you would love to create, regardless of how it makes you feel. When you create goals without attachment to whether it works out or not, ironically, it's more likely to happen. I can give you countless examples of thinking *That would be amazing* and then forgetting about it, only for the outcome to occur while I did very little. Like the time I manifested a TEDx talk, an astral chart reading and an interview on ITV's morning show *This Morning*.

In April 2015, I was sitting in my living room in London after returning from Bali. I was watching ITV's

This Morning and suddenly thought, *It would be so cool to be on this programme!*

I never gave it another thought. Then the next month I found myself on *This Morning* being interviewed on British national television about my book, *Goodbye Mr Ex*.

How did this come about? At the time I had been on a retreat in Lanzarote when, on one of the breaks, I went for a cup of coffee and checked my email. There in my inbox was a message from a journalist I had met years ago in London, asking whether I wanted to be interviewed about infidelity on *This Morning*. In that moment, my insecurity took over and I couldn't see how I was going to fly to London in time for an interview the next day. I told her I couldn't go as I was on a retreat in Lanzarote and I was still breast-feeding my son.

I told my ex-husband and he said I shouldn't pass up on such an extraordinary opportunity. I realised he was right and emailed her immediately to let her know that I would do it. Over the next few hours, the show changed their minds about the content they were going to use, so the plan changed at least three times. At 3 pm I was told it was on!

In a flash I booked a ticket and found myself jetting off to the UK. Luckily, I had bought some formula for our son. He could stay with his dad while I was free to be interviewed. I arrived at 1am and was taken to the hotel by taxi. The next morning ITV paid for me to get into London. The next thing I knew I was sitting next to Denise Robertson, having hair and makeup done and being ushered into the studio. I was interviewed by Amanda Holden and Phillip Schofield before being picked up by a taxi and taken to the airport. I was back in Lanzarote later that day to finish off the retreat in style!

Now, I didn't plan for that. It had been my heartfelt intent (however fleeting) to be on British national television. The opportunity came out of the blue. It seems when you know that these feelings of security and wellbeing are not dependent on the outcome, you are more likely to create it.

What I learned from this is what I call *'Calling It In'*

You see, whatever you want already exists. You can call in whatever you want and aspire to. You don't even need to believe in whether it will come into being: It just needs to be an outcome that you experience with a light heart. In my experience, non-attachment creates the environment for quick manifestation. The less we seem to care about the very thing we want to create, the more likely it is to happen.

The joy of experimentation

But what about those times when you want a result, but it doesn't happen? There is always something you can learn from not achieving the outcome you wanted, right? As far as I can tell, if you come with the attitude of curiosity and exploration and are 'being' (in the present moment), it's easier to experiment without needing the outcome to be as you think it should be.

Have you ever stopped to consider that life is one big experiment?

I hadn't, until I observed my son Leo playing on the beach one day. He was attempting to pick up one of his small toys with a big spade, with the intent of fitting it through a hole that was way too small. As I pointed this out to him, he got upset. I realised that he wasn't attached to the outcome. He was more interested in experimenting with the resources he had, to see what the outcome would be!

Oh wow, what if you could come to work and life this way? How different would your experience of taking action be? Leo wasn't concerned about whether he failed or succeeded. He was interested in what would happen if he did this or that. In short, he was more interested in finding out what would happen if...

What if you could see your work and life as a game? What if you came to both with an attitude of curiosity and fun? Who you become in the process of the experimentation is just as important as the result.

Ideals hinder progress

When you place expectations on something working out and it doesn't in the way you want it to, it can hinder the progress you are seeking. When you focus on the ideal, you may well forgo the wisdom that is there for you to listen to. If you are hell-bent on something needing to be the way you imagined it and are not open to the journey looking different from the way you envisaged, it can hold up the process and keep you in dissatisfaction.

As a hardworking mum I am sure that you are constantly coming up with creative ideas, projects, business ideas, services or even activities for your kids to entertain themselves with. I invite you to see the next story I share as a metaphor for your work and life. You see, I learned a very wise lesson through Leo's birth.

While pregnant with Leo, I wanted a natural birth (outcome). I read every book on the subject and I watched every movie I could find. It never occurred to me that I might need to go to hospital and have a C-section. That wasn't a reality I had ever entertained.

A few days before he was born, I was having a conversation with one of my mentors who shared a story about his ex-wife who, like me, wanted a natural birth but ended with having a C-section. I listened with great interest, but little did I know that the story would come back to help me when giving birth.

Seven days before he was born, I had full-on contractions, but he wasn't ready to come out. I went to see the doctor who told me Leo was in the wrong position and I needed to work my body to get him in the right one.

After six days of contractions, I had done everything possible to move him into the right birthing position. I had a chat with the midwife, and as I spoke to her she caught something that hadn't been in my awareness at all: I had been denying the possibility that I may need to have a C-section. As we spoke, I realised how angry I was at my mother for giving birth to me by C-section and not giving me the experience of being born naturally. I hadn't realised how much anger I carried. Once I acknowledged it and saw through my illusion, I went into labour five hours later.

However, the plan of having a natural birth at home was thwarted when I realised that the best course of action was to go to hospital. It wasn't ideal, but 20 hours later I knew I needed extra help. When we arrived, I was tested to see how dilated I was, and to my dismay I was only five centimetres. An hour later it had gone to seven centimetres, so it all looked like it was heading in the right direction. As I had dilated so quickly, I was curious to find out how long it would take and asked the doctor. He answered that it would it take another five hours based on my current condition. I kept on pushing.

After five hours of pushing, squatting, screaming, panting, breathing and throwing up, the doctor came and broke the news that I was still seven centimetres dilated and nothing had changed! In that moment I knew it was time to surrender. It was the wisest thing to do. As they gave me the epidural, I passed out. When I came around, the doctor had sewn me up and handed baby Leo to his father.

Yes, Leo was born (outcome), but the way in which it happened (C-section) wasn't my ideal (natural birth at home). But progress was made as I had listened to what was needed in each moment. If I'd stuck to the rules and the logic of my intellect, I wouldn't have listened to the intelligence that was there to guide me to safety in a way that was right for me.

In life, as in business and work, things don't necessarily turn out the way we want them to. I usually joke that, "Here is the plan, here is what really happened, and they look nothing alike". While your plans may not progress in the way you want them to, they do not create the feelings you have.

Measuring progress

Do you ever measure progress by looking ahead at how much more you need to do? If I had measured the progress of my birth success by having achieved a natural birth, I would have been sorely disappointed. Have you ever considered that this way of measuring isn't the most accurate way of understanding what you have achieved? It may sound obvious as you read this, but you would be surprised by the number of conversations I have with clients who still measure progress by how much still needs to get done.

The only constructive way to measure progress is to look back at how far you have come. Sometimes we undermine how much we have achieved because even the biggest steps seem small. I also know that it may seem hard to judge how much you have accomplished, when you think you should be further down the line. I invite you to take some time out to jot down ten things you have already achieved in the past year. You may amaze yourself!

As you look at what you have achieved, you may even see that getting there was actually quite effortless. If it wasn't, and what you achieved (or didn't) doesn't sit right with you now, consider whether you set toxic goals or heartfelt intentions. Most likely the actions based on heartfelt intentions were effortless and brought you joy. So how to do more of what you love and what brings you joy especially if you just feel SO BUSY? Well, now it's time to learn how to create time and space!

Let's recap and reflect

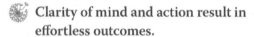 Clarity of mind and action result in effortless outcomes.

There is value in failure because what you learn and who you become in the process is priceless.

Set goals if you want to.

Your goals cannot make you happy, so you may as well set some cool intentions.

Experiment, experiment, experiment!

Fuel progress by flowing with the changes that life has in store for you.

Measure your progress by looking back, not by how far you need to go.

CHAPTER TEN

Creating More Time and Space

*"We are living in a culture entirely hypnotised
by the illusion of time."*

ALAN WATTS

Do you constantly feel that the clock is always against you? If so, you are not alone. Most of the hardworking, busy mums I have worked with tell me the same thing: "I just don't have the time". If this sounds familiar then welcome to creating more space for it!

In this chapter, I want to challenge the time myths that will be keeping you from creating more of it. You may need more time to do the housework, finish that project or have special time with your kids. My intention with this chapter is to share my insights into the subject of time, with the purpose of you enjoying more of it.

The illusion of time

Over the past few years, I have seen how time is really an illusion. It expands and contracts depending on your state of mind. Do you have days where it feels like time speeds up or slows down, where the same 60 minutes can feel like an eternity or flash past in the blink of an eye? If so, you are not alone.

Time is a concept learned as children. Leo has no concept of time and doesn't understand what tomorrow is yet. In fact, children don't understand the concept of it until they are about six years old. That is why we have to start with how many sleeps it will take until he sees his dad or goes somewhere. In Leo's world, there is no future – only now. Even if we have the capacity to catapult ourselves into the future and bring up the past, these are illusions of time created by our imagination.

Have you noticed that when time seems to go by quickly, it is when your mind is all revved up? It may look like time is running out – that you won't make that deadline, that the project you need to get done won't be finished in time and so on. But when you come back, just being in the present, time seems to move slower, giving you the sense of it expanding. You can feel like you can actually get more done in the time you have – and you do!

However, when you are busy filling your time with work, meetings, children, shopping, cooking or whatever else you do to cover the basics, it may feel that you don't have any time left. So what do you do instead? You decide to multitask to save time.

Research shows that multitasking doesn't work, even if you are a woman![3] In fact, you can waste a lot of time because of errors made by lack of focus. Is there any wonder that you fall into the trap of checking your phone or answering that last email as you hang out with those you love? This is the mind's way of saying, *I want to distract you from the present moment!* This sort of habitual thinking will rob you of being fully present.

Your relationship to thinking about time

Have you found there are days where you don't do as much yet accomplish a lot? And there are days where you are really busy but accomplish very little? Have you ever wondered what is going on? I can tell you that it has nothing to do with the length of your to-do list but more to do with how you relate to time or, rather, the relationship with the thinking you have about time.

How you show up on the inside is usually a reflection of how you are on the outside.

If you have a busy mind, you will probably find that your experience of your days is busy. Is there any wonder that your days seem so hectic? If you experience your days with frantic thinking, you will experience them as frantic.

I remember when I lived in Hertfordshire and travelled in and out of London all the time. For some

[3] Merrill Douglas, Forbes, *Why Multitasking Doesn't Work* https://www.forbes.com/sites/douglasmerrill/2012/08/17/why-multitasking-doesnt-work/#132df83c6ada, 17 Aug, 2012

reason, I thought I had to. I would run around like a blue-arsed fly being busy but getting little done. In fact, I lived in a world with so much revved-up thinking that I was burning myself out as I went from meeting to meeting, from potential client to potential client, without giving myself the time and space I needed to slow down and take time for quiet reflection.

In this day and age, being busy has come to be something the Western world reveres. If you are not being busy then you are somehow lazy and no longer part of the biggest club in the working world – the Busy Club.

But why have you fallen for busy? Why do you keep saying yes to rushing around?

The simple answer is that we don't know any better. It's innocent. It's a habit of thinking that has turned into a habit of action. We see others do it, and we think that's how we can achieve and get what we want from our work, business and life. Logically, it makes sense that if you are being busy, you will achieve more, but this isn't true. I know it's counterintuitive, but what if you were to realise that *slowing down is the key to making more time for yourself and getting better results*?

In fact, as you may have discovered, it's difficult to be quiet and reflective when you are constantly busy 'inside'. Is it any wonder there are so many people attempting to treat their busy mind with overwork and mobile phones because they can't switch off?

Being busy becomes a habit – someone that you are. But behaviours are not who we are. Clues may lie in the name we have given ourselves – human BE-ings as opposed to human DO-ings.

One of my insights into the addiction of 'busy' is that we use it as a clever distraction to avoid insecure thought. It's an incredible strategy that may work for a while, but over time it can lead to burnout and even more stress.

Switching off and slowing down

Switching off is a great idea, but have you ever considered that it's impossible to switch thoughts off – to stop thinking? The more you attempt to switch off and not think, the more thinking you will probably experience. You cannot suppress thoughts and the more you attempt to resist them, the more they will persist. If I ask you not to think of a green banana, I'm sure that all you can now see is a green banana! The more energy you bring to the thoughts you don't want, the more judgment you bring to them, the bigger they become and the more they may disturb you.

You may have been using a glass of wine, running or putting on a movie at night as the answer to coping with the busy and hardworking day you've had. Correlation is not causation. Just because two things correlate doesn't mean that one causes the other. I know it's logical to believe that the activity is the cause of the switching off, but just because it happens doesn't mean it is the reason. Have there been times when you went for a run or drank that wine only to find it didn't help? I have. So it's not the run. It's not the wine. It's something else.

What if, instead of wanting to empty your mind or stop thinking by doing an activity, you could see that the stillness and calm you seek is innate? It isn't something you need to do an activity for, but rather it is something that exists 'inside' already.

A key to experiencing the space within it is to slow down.

The Spanish say, "Visteme despacio, porque quiero ir deprisa", which means "Dress me slowly, I am in a hurry". When you slow down, counter intuitively it can speed you up. Rushing around and going fast can often lead to mistakes and careless actions, which may end up creating more work and more headaches for you.

Instead, when you move at a slower pace, it reveals the space within that already exists. As you experience more stillness and calm, it offers up new habits of behaviour that are in line with your internal experience. Don't be surprised if you start to enjoy taking breaks and make time for quiet reflection and 'off' time to naturally create more space in your day. You will inevitably be more productive because you are less distracted, more focused and immersed in what you are doing as you bring presence of mind to your activities.

When you have less on your mind, you are able to focus far more. You bring presence of mind to the activity you are doing and become immersed in it. This can give you back a lot of time as it's the distracted mind that takes you out of flow and focus. Mind chatter has incredible pull to take you out of the present moment, especially if you buy into the 'just let me do this before I...'

I am sure you've experienced times when you've been on your way to the kitchen to grab a cup of tea or coffee and you've spotted things that needed doing along the way, like picking laundry off the floor or putting away the Lego. By the time you get to the kitchen you've forgotten all about making tea and have got on with doing the washing up, right?

I know it's compelling to do what the chatter tells us, but is it really necessary for you to do all of that before making a cup of tea? It probably looks that way, but it's also possible to just make the cup of tea without acting on what the mental chatter is telling you. Is there any wonder you aren't able to put your feet up with all that internal distraction? You end up doing more to compensate for the time you have lost.

Conversely, I am sure you've had times where you are so deeply immersed in the present moment that you have lost all sense of time and space. This is what some would call the 'flow state' – a state of meditation where you go beyond the body and senses and don't even notice what's going on around you. Athletes and musicians talk about being in the Zone – a peak performance state. It's natural to experience life in this way as it is innate. What takes you out of it is the gravitational pull of your internal chatter.

A few years ago, I was creating 21 videos for a Facebook challenge – The 21 Day Effortless Experience. On the first day it took me three hours to produce three five-minute videos. The next day I managed to film all 21 in one take over a three-hour period. This enabled me to catch up on the time I had lost the previous day, and it left me with the rest of the day to enjoy myself!

So what happened?

The first day my mind was distracted by the internal judgments about the videos I was shooting. The next day, however, I was in flow and immersed in the action as my innate clarity and joy had been restored. There was space for the message to come through me, which in turn sped up the process.

Priorities and work/life balance

As it is your relationship to your thinking about time that is at play here, the way you prioritise your time will be impacted by it too. Have you noticed that you always have time for things that you make time for? Do you have time for...

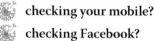 checking your mobile?

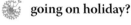 checking Facebook?

going on holiday?

If you said yes to any of these, you *do* have time to prioritise what *you* want to spend time on. If you don't know what your priorities are, take some time out to reflect on what they might be for your work and personal life. Here are some questions to consider.

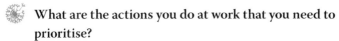 **What are the actions you do at work that you need to prioritise?**

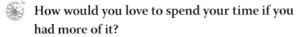 **How would you love to spend your time if you had more of it?**

What matters most to you, and how can you create more time for it/them?

There are many ways to skin a cat, but for me it started with a desire to create more time for my health, family and friends. This is when wisdom nudged and guided me to create more of the life I was yearning for, which I believed that I had no time for. This is why searching for the perfect work/life balance doesn't work. You heard me right.

If you keep searching for THE perfect work/life balance, all this does is keep you in searching mode, which won't help you find it.

One thing I have observed on my Discovery Calls (where I see if a potential client and I are a good fit), is that 90 per cent of the time the topic of work/life balance shows up. They feel that life is more about work than play. They say they haven't found the perfect balance and keep searching for it, like a dog chasing its own tail.

They tend to have spent a lot of their time attempting to manage their time tools and beat themselves up when they don't use them or when their work leaks into family time by checking, answering emails and taking calls. While there is nothing inherently wrong with this, in beating themselves up they are moving away from the joy and peace of mind they seek.

If you think the amount of time you spend in your work and personal life has anything to do with how much joy you will feel, you are innocently mistaken. Everyone has the right to choose how they fill their time, and that will be unique to you. But attempting to quench a desire by balancing out the amount of time you spend on one thing or another is futile.

If you were to notice where you put pressure on yourself to have the life you strive for, and you listened more closely to what you are being drawn to, you may find that the life you desire happens naturally.

Personally, I never searched for the work/life balance holy grail. But because I've spent more time in the stillness and calm, I have naturally found that working long hours without taking time out doesn't make any sense. I now have a diary that isn't full, and I always ensure I get enough me-time in there too. Time exists and is ever present, but how you experience it will be as a result of thought. As the mind settles, spending time on helpful activities will make more sense.

To create more time and space, you don't have to be a wonder woman. Remember, that time is an illusion and how you utilise it has so much to do with how you relate to it and think about it. You don't have to set goals if you don't want to. You don't need to just rush towards them, set them at the expense of yourself. Set priorities – and you are the biggest! Now, as you explore these new ways of being, the mummy-guilt will most likely raise its head. We'll discover more about that voice in the next chapter.

Let's recap and reflect

- Time is an illusion and will go quicker or slower depending on your state of mind.

- Past and future is conceptual and something we learn at a young age.

- It's your relationship to thinking about time that will give you more or less of it.

- Being busy is indicative of your state of mind.

- Attempting to switch off will only create more noise.

- No activity will help you switch off.

- A distracted mind will rob you of time.

- Flow is innate and will create more time.

- Live life the way it works for you.

CHAPTER ELEVEN

Self-care in the Face of Guilt

"It takes a village to raise a child."

AFRICAN PROVERB

Most of us today don't live where we grew up. With the explosion of technology and the opportunities it has brought about with regards to work, more and more mums find themselves bringing up their children with less support than before. Back in the day, families used to share the responsibilities of bringing up children in the village of their birth. Is there any wonder that mums today struggle with the juggle of work, running a business, looking after kids and looking after themselves too?

When it comes to joy and living more, looking after your own wellbeing is the best way to experience more of it. A by-product of slowing down and experiencing more stillness is that you will want to take more care of your state of mind and your body. As a working mum, I know the norm is to give and give and give to everyone else and attend to others (especially if you have small children). But the only way to ensure that the giving is sustainable is to be 'selfish' and look after you – your self.

Nevertheless, the beliefs that keep most mums from looking after themselves, both mentally and physically, are that they have 'no time' and that 'self-care is an indulgence'. As you read in the last chapter, you do have time. You just need to make your self-care and happiness your number one priority. To do that, you need to choose 'you' first above your work, your kids and those you love.

Nourish you first and everything else around you will flourish.

Looking after your state of mind

Have you noticed that when you are grounded (in touch with reality), everyone around you responds differently? That's because you are like a tuning fork. Most mums I work with underestimate the power they have to influence those around them, especially their children. Children look to model others, particularly their parents. If they see their parents experiencing the ups and downs with grace, it will help them to self-regulate with more ease.

I'm sure that when you are tired, stressed and overwhelmed, you may act out or be less patient with your kids and those you love. If you are anything like me, you may feel shame for the way you act. You beat yourself up. As far as I can tell, it doesn't help anyone, least of all the very people you want to support – your kids. You then feel guilty, and the feeling perpetuates.

Before being a mum, I had heard other mums talk about mum guilt, but I didn't think it would be something I'd ever experience. I should have known better. As someone who had misread what guilt was saying about work, of course I would do the same with the way I was taking care of Leo. It seems that when you become a mum, guilt becomes a rite of passage.

On the surface, guilt is saying you should spend more time working on your projects or more time at work to meet the deadlines. You know this because when you take time out, you feel guilty. Or perhaps it looks to you as if guilt means you are not a good mum because you did something you aren't proud of, and you're worried you're not doing the right thing for your kids.

All the mums I've supported in their efforts to fall back in love with life are doing an amazing job. The only thing that gets in the way of them seeing that is the guilt they beat themselves with. Guilt is a feeling that only knows about *the state of mind you are in* and knows nothing about whether you are a doing a good job or not.

You are only ever doing what makes sense to you in the moment. As you have no control over how your child will perceive you, you might as well reach out for compassion and kindness for 'you' instead.[4] The best thing we can do for anyone is to 'bring the feeling home'.

Bring the feeling home

What do I mean by 'bringing the feeling home'? It is something I heard at a seminar in London that was part of a year-long state-of-mind programme. It was during this seminar that Leo's nanny sent me a picture of the two of them on the beach. I felt so guilty about having left my 18-month-old and had all these judgmental thoughts rush in to tell me what a bad mother I was for having left him there.

I must have spent the entire day going in and out of that feeling of guilt, until we all sat down to listen to a Sydney Banks recording.[5] About 10 minutes in, I heard him say: "All you need to do is bring the feeling home". What I heard in that was: *All I need to do is look after my own joy and wellbeing, which actually helps everyone else.* It's not about how much time I spend with Leo, it's about the feeling I am 'in' when I am with him. All the judgments I had about this aspect of motherhood dropped away.

As it turned out, Leo had an amazing time that weekend! So there was nothing to worry about.

---

[4] If you need extra resources on guilt-free living, see my Free Bonus at the back of this book.

[5] Sydney Banks was a Scottish welder who had an epiphany about how life works and went on to share his wisdom all over the world, waking people up to this truth.

Discover and do what brings you joy

While joy is inside, there will be activities in your life that will make your heart sing. Have you forgotten what these are? If so, I invite you to reflect on the activities you used to do as a child, or activities you used to love but stopped doing because of all the responsibilities you have. For me, it used to be singing. When I rediscovered my joy for it, I decided to join a rock choir.

For my VIP client Michelle it was painting. In fact, when she realised that she had been putting it off to make money, she stopped and decided to make it a priority. As a result, she has now illustrated a book and been commissioned to do bespoke pieces. Once you discover what your heart wants you to express in the way you want to express it, you can.

What if you didn't need to take your guilt so seriously? Would this enable you to put 'you' as the priority and spend less time at work and more time doing the things you love? What I have observed in the years of helping working mums fall back in love with life is that they put off doing the very activities that bring them joy. This is because they feel guilty and believe they feel this way because they should go from working hard to going home and tending to their families. They put off doing what makes their hearts sing.

In some cases, they have been so wrapped in the 'once I have x amount in the bank, I will do y' or 'once my child is... I will do x' that they have forgotten what activities outside work and family life bring them joy. Activities like going for a massage, to the spa, dancing, singing, going for walk, doing a yoga class or just drinking a cup of tea in silence, all get put on the 'I know I should but—' pile. And weirdly enough, the very activities that bring them joy become an obligation and something else that perceptively brings on a guilt trip.

It doesn't have to be that way for them – or for you! You can make these pursuits a priority and let everything else support them. I understand that you may need to have a conversation with your other half about this (if you have one). If you are concerned about rocking the boat, don't be. My clients tell me time and again that once they make the commitment to take time off and 'ask' for it, they discover it's a conversation that needed to happen anyway.

Sharing that you need time out isn't something you need to be afraid of or feel shame over – it's your birthright. Once the other people involved experience you as a happier and more relaxed human being, my guess is they will want you to do more of it!

I have also discovered that when you are in a relaxed state of mind, your best ideas and solutions appear. You never know where your joy will lead you, just as Michelle woke up to her love for painting and is now being paid for her gift.

Schedule joy time

One of the main barriers stopping my busy clients from doing what they love is not scheduling me-time in the diary. I've noticed that if I don't put something in the diary, it doesn't happen. Have you found that too?

I know for a busy mum it's often easy to make clients or kids a priority and have your own activities overlooked. But it is possible to include you in the diary too! Block your diary out as you wish to design your week, and you will be amazed at what happens. When you schedule me-time in the diary, it means that the time slot is taken. By doing this, you are firming up boundaries and generating the time you said you didn't have for your self-care.

Here are some key questions that may help you in doing this. They helped when I was letting work and child time leak into the me-time I so desperately needed.

 What am I not willing to compromise on?

If I could design my week to look the way I want, what would it look like?

When you schedule the time you need for 'you' within the parameters of what is possible, you are saying yes to you. This may mean saying no to others. It might feel intimidating, but it doesn't need to be.

Boundaries: The art of saying no

Saying no may seem rude or selfish, but there really is nothing wrong with it. Boundaries and being able to say no helps others too. It allows others to increase their level of understanding of what works for you and what doesn't. Saying no, sharing your truth and stating what works for you, what you can and cannot do, is so important if you want to design the me-time you need.

Putting boundaries in place doesn't have to be nasty or done in a horrible way. You can explain that it's something you need and is important to you. Have you ever considered that saying no can actually benefit those you are saying it to? Let me explain.

If you say yes to everything all the time, can you give to someone else the way you want to when you are spread so thin? I know it's easy for the people pleaser to come out and play, but it's okay to disappoint other people. The way they respond to you isn't personal. It's telling you how they are experiencing their own thinking in the moment.

As with everything in life, you just need to start. The more times you do it, even if your attempts are clunky, the easier it will be and the more comfortable you will become with doing it over time.

I have also discovered that saying yes when you want to say no will take you further away from joy and may well let the resentful thoughts creep in. Let me give you an example.

Last year I ran my *Effortless Business Program*. In my mind's eye, what I really wanted to do was run it during the day so that I wouldn't have to take late-night calls and miss out on quality time with my son. But I let my boundaries slip again. There were a couple of ladies who said they could only take part if it was in the evenings. I changed my mind to fit in around them! This was a massive learning experience for me. I learned that the women who said they couldn't make it during the day ended up leaving the program! I was left with a time that didn't work for me, and they left anyway!

When we say no to the things that don't work for us, we put a stake in the ground that people are more likely to adhere to. When you commit to your boundaries, it doesn't matter whether someone else is not happy with it. What is important is that you are free to do what is right for you and not to act out of fear because you think you might upset someone. Besides, even if there is a misunderstanding, where they experience upset, it can be an opportunity for deeper connection.

Ask for help

Another way to expand your self-care time is to ask for help. Often we think we need to pay someone for this extra help, but it's not true. I am sure there are friends and family that can help you out, if you only ask.

To ask for help isn't a sign of weakness. We often mistake asking for help as burdening others. But have you ever considered that asking for help could be a gift for someone else? Human beings love to help. It's in our nature. But often we don't ask for it because subconsciously we have a problem with receiving it. Do you?

If asking for help and being open to receiving it is something you find uncomfortable, I invite you to notice the feeling and get curious about it. The chances are you were educated with beliefs that made asking for help into something you shouldn't do: *You should manage alone.* The fact that you were rewarded in the past for doing it yourself entrenches the belief further and compounds the existing behaviour. As with saying no, the more you ask for help, the easier it will become!

You can make self-care a priority despite the mum guilt. Discover the things that you love and that bring you joy – and do them. Slot them into your diary and say no to things, events and people who interfere with that. Remember, your attitude to time will help you manage it. You actually have all the time in the world! Come back to your 'home' within at any time. The stillness, the insights are always there.

To ask for help isn't a sign of weakness.

Let's recap and reflect

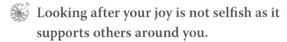 Looking after your joy is not selfish as it supports others around you.

You don't have to buy into mum-guilt as it's not saying anything about you.

Bring the feeling home.

Discover what makes your heart sing as it is your birthright.

Do what brings you joy.

Schedule joy time in your diary.

Create boundaries to do what is right for you.

Ask for and receive the help.

Drawing the Journey to a Close

We have come to the end of our journey together. And as with every ending there will always be a new beginning. Your new beginning starts now. It starts by knowing that the 'Joy of Being' is possible for you. It is possible to navigate your life with more joy because who you are can never be touched by the outside world. Any feeling you have ever felt, good or bad, has only ever come from 100 per cent of thinking in that given moment.

The implications of this to your work and life are enormous. If you cannot feel what is 'out there', you are more likely to remain calm in the eye of the storm. You know that your wellbeing and security lies deep inside, and consequently, you will experience your life with more love and understanding.

As you spend less time in stress and overwhelm, insecurity falls away and insight keeps pointing you back to where your experience comes from. You will begin to observe the thoughts you experience and stop taking them so seriously, and unhelpful habits of thinking and behaviour fall away. You don't need techniques or methods to save you. Your true nature is infinite and goes far beyond what you think. Thoughts are transient in nature; they come and go like clouds in the sky. By insightfully seeing that you live in a thought-generated reality, you don't need to delve into the content of thinking to find solutions.

To be human is to be alive, experiencing the life you were gifted. Feelings are useful. They let you know which direction you are looking in, which is why you don't need to get rid of the 'negative' ones. They let you know whether you are bringing presence of mind to the moment. This is useful to know because, without these signposts dressed up as feelings, you wouldn't be able to experience life. The challenge that humanity is up against is not that we experience stress and anxiety, but that we think something other than thought is creating these feelings. When you accept that your state of mind is in a constant state of flux, you know the low periods will pass.

As you discover who you really are and what you are made of, you begin to define your preference for which world you'd rather spend more time in. As you go inside and see through your own limited and past conditioning, you will notice the space within, which in turn allows you to *be* more.

As you experience more of this stillness and peace, you will begin to notice even more space:

- You won't react to things as you did before because you will have time to respond.
- You will swap judgments for curiosity.
- You will find yourself becoming more present to others and to the moment.
- Harshness will be replaced by softness and hate by compassion.
- Internal struggles will be replaced by ease and grace, more of the time.

In short, stillness brings joy.

The more space you inhabit internally, the more enticing slowing down and stopping will be for you. Rushing about and being frantic for the sake of it will be less appealing and your self-care will become a more usual activity.

You will tend to be far more productive and effective and find that you have more time for the things you love. After all, you can now decide effortlessly to make more time for them. Time will expand and shrink depending on your experience, but you can help yourself by asking for the help you need, safe in the knowledge that you deserve to be supported. Time or lack of it will become less of a concern as you realise that it's an internal experience.

As you gain clarity and are better able to discern what is wrong and right for you, you can say no without guilt and yes to the experiences you once didn't think you deserved. You are free to live your life and conduct your business the way you want, rather than being at the mercy of what you feel or the people around you.

You are free to be the most fully self-expressed version of you without needing to apologise for it.

This newfound confidence is the intangible asset that will help you to see opportunities and enable you to take action on your bright ideas.

The Joy of Being is a way of being, and specifically in this case, a way of being in the present moment. When you experience life from right *now*, there is nothing you need to change as you already have everything you need in this moment.

Keep looking in the direction of what creates your experience and life becomes easier to navigate. Driving a car looking in the direction of travel is easier than driving whilst looking through the rear-view mirror. As insecure thought drops away, you can listen to that inner voice more clearly and life doesn't look like such an uphill struggle after all.

You can relax as insight will do the heavy lifting for you. It will help you see through the illusions that have been making life seem difficult. Wisdom will help to soothe moments of darkness and your internal GPS system will guide you. Any answer you ever searched for is hidden in the true self, in the space within.

But wisdom doesn't always look pretty. It doesn't always come in the form of marshmallows and hot chocolate with coloured sprinkles on top. It can sometimes come disguised as divorce, death, deception, injury or illness. By knowing that joy exists and that your experience is an inside job, perceived tragic happenings can be experienced with more grace and you will bounce back more quickly by spending less time in the doldrums.

You have the capacity for insight, which means you will never stop having them until the day you die. You will find the answers you are looking for, always. They will arrive when they are good and ready.

Wisdom supports you to get results and manifest what you want. The unknown doesn't look as frightening as it did before, and you act regardless of where it may lead or how you feel. Your path will become apparent as you notice nudges, signs and curiosity guiding you.

There is nowhere to get to and nowhere to be – searching is an option. You don't need to be enslaved by feelings of 'not enoughness'. *More* is an illusory destination that you will never get to, so it's okay to enjoy your life *right now* regardless of your circumstances. You are more resilient than you think, more capable than you think and so much more than you think. You are not separate from life: You are life 'lifeing'.

Life is one big experiment. Your work, the way you parent and play are creative expressions of you, so why not play full out? You may not get the outcomes you wished for, but that's okay. Who you become and what you learn along the way, are all part of the process. Joy is your birthright, and it's possible for you – for everyone – to experience life's beauty and magic no matter the circumstances by looking inside. The Joy of Being is in your hands right now.

Free Bonus Support

If you need extra resources to support you on your Joy of Being journey, please accept a gift of a free download of my Guilt Free Living audio on the www.MarinaPearson.com homepage. Or listen to the Joy of Being podcast episode 27 www. MarinaPearson.com/podcast where I interview Ruth Douglas about guilt-free mothering.

Bibliography

Banks, Sydney (5), *The Missing Link, Reflections on Philosophy and Spirit*, USA: Lone Pine Publishing (CA); 2nd ed. edition (15 September 2016)

Frankl, Victor, *Man's Search for Meaning*, Beacon Press, Boston USA, (June 2006)

Maharaj, Sri Nisargadatta, *I AM THAT,* Chetana Private Ltd; 4 Revised edition (5 December 1999)

Neill, Michael, *The Space (Within): Finding Your Way Back Home*, USA: Hay House (May 2016)

Neill, Michael, *The Inside-Out Revolution,* Hay House, UK (6 May 2013)

Smart, Jamie, *Clarity: Clear Mind, Better Performance, Bigger Results*, UK: Capstone (26 February 2013)

Smart, Jamie, Results: *Think Less. Achieve More.* UK: Capstone; 1st edition (5 December 2016)

Watts, W. Alan, *Quotable Quote*, GoodReads, https://www.goodreads.com/quotes/374572-we-are-living-in-a-culture-entirely-hypnotized-by-the

Emerson, Waldo Ralph, GoodReads, https://www.goodreads.com/quotes/15579-what-lies-behind-us-and-what-lies-before-us-are

Merrill Douglas, Forbes, Why Multitasking Doesn't Work https://www.forbes.com/sites/douglasmerrill/2012/08/17/why-multitasking-doesnt-work/#132df83c6ada, (17 August 2012)

About the Author

Marina Pearson is a mother, bestselling author, international TEDx speaker, investor and Joy Retreat facilitator. Most of all she is a human Be-ing. She lives her life working on projects that light her up and in the process assists others to also light up their lives.

Over 14 years' experience in the transformation industry has culminated in Marina helping mums to ditch the stress at the Joy Retreats she hosts from her home in Javea, Spain.

As host of the *Joy of Being* podcast, Marina interviews transformation professionals, business owners and creatives on how to live a life we can truly enjoy.

Marina's work has been featured on ITV's *This Morning*, *Marie Claire*, *Spirit & Destiny*, *The Guardian* and the *Daily Mail*. She is also the bestselling author of *Goodbye Mr Ex*.

If you are interested in finding out where your joy gaps are and what you can do about them, visit:

www.MarinaPearson.com/scorecard.

You can also join Marina on the *Joy of Being* podcast at www.MarinaPearson.com/podcast.